Advanced 1

"A brilliant evidence-based guide that Dr. Woodstein has sensitively combined her extensive knowledge with the voices and experiences of LGBTQ+ parents to produce a nuanced guide that will support many on their journey of starting, extending and blending their families. A must read for LGBTQ+ parents and anyone who works in pregnancy, birth and parenting support."

—Amy Brown, author of *The Positive Breastfeeding Book*

"As B.J. says, all parents have the right to feel seen and accepted. It's the responsibility of everyone who works with LGBTQ+ families to educate themselves and to step up to ensure that they offer support and empathy. This book is a great place to start. By sharing stories, as well as detailed factual information, this book makes an essential contribution to the education of professionals and volunteers."

—Emma Pickett, IBCLC, author of *The Breast Book*

"B.J.'s book is inclusive, careful and positive. It contains first hand accounts from parents from all backgrounds, so you can hear how people have managed and why they made the choices they did. This book will also be invaluable for birthing and childcare professionals from medicine, education, health and care, to gain an insight into this small but rising family formation."

—Dr. Finn Mackay, author of *Female Masculinities and the Gender Wars*

We're Here!

A Practical Guide to Becoming an LGBTQ+ Parent

B.J. Woodstein

Praeclarus Press, LLC
©2022 B.J. Woodstein.

www.PraeclarusPress.com

Praeclarus Press, LLC
2504 Sweetgum Lane
Amarillo, Texas 79124 USA
806-367-9950
www.PraeclarusPress.com

DISCLAIMER

The information contained in this publication is advisory only and is not intended to replace sound clinical judgment or individualized patient care. The author disclaims all warranties, whether expressed or implied, including any warranty as the quality, accuracy, safety, or suitability of this information for any particular purpose.

ISBN: 978-1-946665-54-6

©2022 B.J. Woodstein

Cover Design: Ken Tackett
Developmental Editing: Kathleen Kendall-Tackett
Copyediting: Chris Tackett
Layout & Design: Nelly Murariu

Dedication

To Fi, Esther, and Tovah, with all my love.

Acknowledgements

I would like to start by thanking all the LGBTQ+ parents who shared their stories with me; some of those experiences are included in what follows. I know it wasn't always easy for you to discuss your personal and often emotional journeys. I learned from all of you, and I appreciate you trusting me with your family narratives. Thank you, too, to the professionals who were willing to speak to me about their work with LGBTQ+ parents, and who showed a desire to support us to the best of their ability.

I also feel inspired by and grateful to all the LGBTQ+ people, past and present, who have fought for rights and for visibility, and who have helped bring us to the point where we have so many possible options for becoming parents.

At Praeclarus Press, Ken Tackett was willing to take a chance on this book. He provided support and ideas, including the title for the book, as well as the beautiful cover. Kathleen Kendall-Tackett offered useful feedback on an early draft.

Finally, I am, as ever, thankful for my amazing wife, Fi, and our fantastic children, Esther and Tovah. I feel lucky to live in a time and place where Fi and I could marry, as well as produce and raise children together, and I hope that more LGBTQ+ people around the world will have this opportunity in the near future. My life is full and happy because I get to spend each day with Fi, Esther, and Tovah. Thank you for being who you are.

Thank you to everyone who participated in the making of this book and to those who read it.

Table of Contents

Section 4 - Feeding

SECTION 1

Overview

Introduction

We're here, we're queer, and we're parents!

More and more people who identify as lesbian, gay, bisexual, trans, and queer (LGBTQ+, but more information on terminology in just a moment) are having children, and that means that we're changing how society defines and understands what a family can look like. This is incredibly exciting, although it can also be confusing for some people and downright challenging for others.

It can also be bewildering on a pragmatic level for those who are LGBTQ+ because there are many ways to make a family and it isn't easy to find lists of pros and cons for different methods. Adoption or surrogacy? Home insemination or at a clinic? Known donor or anonymous? Even once someone is pregnant, the questions continue. Where to give birth? Who will be at the birth? Who will feed the baby and how? What will the baby call the various adults involved in their conception and rearing? Who can or should be on the birth certificate? What rights do the different people have? Who's getting parental leave? How will you parent? How will you explain your queer family to others? This book offers information on these topics and more, helping you think through the options and decide what's right for you. What's right for you may not be what's right for your friends or your relatives, and you may get comments or questions, but if there's one thing us queers know about, it's doing things our own way.

While this book aims to directly serve the LGBTQ+ community by exploring a variety of practical and emotional issues around queer parenting, it is also important that LGBTQ+ people who are on their path to parenting are met by friendly, knowledgeable professionals. For that reason, this book also is intended to be informative for doctors, midwives, doulas, peer supporters, charity workers, breastfeeding/chestfeeding counsellors, lactation consultants, social workers, lawyers, and anyone else who works with parents or people who want to become parents. I believe most people want to be inclusive

3

and supportive, but many don't quite know where to start, so I give you some ideas and suggestions here. In a chapter written specifically for you, I cover everything from pronouns to jealousy, from medical issues to polite ways of asking for information, with the hope that it will arm you with more knowledge about how to better serve this group of people.

In short, I've tried to produce an accessible guide to planning a family for LGBTQ+ people, and for people who work with those who identify as LGBTQ+. But why did I, in particular, write it? Well, I'm LGBTQ+ myself; the label I prefer is queer. My wife and I have two children and often describe ourselves as a two-mum family (we live in the UK, so we say mum). When we were starting on our family-creation journey, I often wished there was a manual that listed our options and explained why people might choose one over another. We talked to friends and joined groups on social media, and I found it helpful to hear people's stories, but I wanted the personal stories to be connected to the practical information. So I decided to write the book that I would have appreciated having.

In addition, I'm an academic, doula, and international board-certified lactation consultant (IBCLC), and I try to meet all the people I support in a way that makes them feel seen and accepted (I don't always succeed, because I'm human, but that is my goal). I've written articles and blog posts, and given lectures and workshops about increasing inclusivity, equality, and an understanding of diversity in the worlds of birth and infant feeding, and I wanted to share this knowledge with others. I have noticed a real increase in the past few years to the number of professionals wanting to serve LGBTQ+ individuals better and to LGBTQ+ people themselves demanding fair and equal treatment, so I think the time is right for discussing LGBTQ+ parenting in depth.

I hope you'll find this book beneficial. Feel free to get in touch with me at lgbtqguidebook@gmail.com if you'd like to share your own stories.

Good luck to you!

A Note on the Personal Stories

This book contains over 40 personal stories, illustrating the various topics discussed here with real-life experiences. I aimed to include as many different tales as I could. Since we're all individuals and we each have our own paths, I probably haven't featured a story that is exactly like your own, but I have tried to include a range of LGBTQ+ experiences to the best of my ability.

Many people gave me access to intimate thoughts, feelings, and details from their own lives, and they chose to do this in order to offer information and to make things better for the next generation of LGBTQ+ people. While some of the contributors use their real names, others use pseudonyms, and some wanted to be anonymous; I have purposely chosen not to include any other identifying details. I recognize that it could have been fascinating and beneficial to acknowledge intersectionality and to hear more about the people featured here—including facts about their ethnicity, religion, education, career, class, location, neurodiversity, ability, background, and so forth—but I was worried that it could make them too easily identifiable or that it would require too much labor on their part to explore all of these topics. Most of them did tell me what term they used to describe their sexuality and/or gender, but some chose not to; if they did do this, I have included their chosen terms.

To find people who were willing to share their tales, I used my own contacts, I posted on social media, and I asked friends, other doulas and lactation consultants, and other people involved in queer activism if they could pass on information about the book. In a few cases, people told me it could be harmful to themselves or their families if they spoke openly about being queer parents, and it's important that we recognize that, for some, it is still hard, traumatic, or anxiety-inducing to be visible and honest about being LGBTQ+ and about being queer parents. I acknowledge the emotional labor that is often required from LGBTQ+ people just to be able to live our lives. I made small edits to grammar or spelling and sometimes broke the stories into different sections, but otherwise did not make substantive changes to them.

A few of the contributors shared information about different aspects of LGBTQ+ family-formation and parenting, so you will notice that they appear multiple times in this book, in different sections. A large number of additional people got in touch with me to share their stories, but sometimes they had similar experiences to others who were already included or else they sent me their stories too late for me to add them in, so I apologize if you contacted me but don't see your work here.

I want this book to feel like a safe space for those who contributed to it and those who are reading it. This means that I didn't want people to be able to figure out who the contributors are or to try to contact them, which is why I only use first names (this is, of course, not the case for the professionals who agreed to write for the book and who happily used their full names). It also means that I hope you, the reader, will feel accepted and welcome here, no matter who you are, what your background is, or how you have created or plan to create your family.

To close this note, I just want to emphasize, again, how grateful I am to all the people who agreed to have their stories in this book. I believe you'll learn a lot from the tales included here. It is not always easy to be open about your experiences, and I know that for a few of the contributors, writing was a challenge, in some cases because it reminded them of painful or difficult times. But they all did it because they wanted to help other LGBTQ+ people. For this, I am truly thankful.

Terminology

I don't feel I can write about LGBTQ+ people and topics without pausing for a moment over terminology. By LGBTQ+, I am referring to lesbian, gay, bisexual, trans, queer, kink, intersex, non-binary, genderqueer, asexual, aromantic, pansexual, throuple (a relationship with three people), polyamorous, non-monogamous, and more. Despite that long list of terms, I know there are others out there too that I've not included on the list, either out of ignorance, because they are less common, or because they might be viewed as a subgroup. If you consider yourself to be LGBTQ+, then you are naturally included.

Also, when it comes to parenting specifically, some people might use terms such as rainbow family[1] or two-mom (or two-mum) family or two-dad family. But, you know, we are also just families and don't always need to have the queer descriptor added on.

I know that some people who identify with the meaning behind some of those terms do not identify with the LGBTQ+ acronym or want to be included under the queer umbrella, while some who do identify as LGBTQ+ wouldn't necessarily include all the other identities under the same heading. To add to that, terminology differs among circumstances, countries, cultures, and time periods, and that affects how people identify and who they feel an affinity with. Put simply, there's a lot of debate about terminology, and our understanding of identity continues to develop and shift. By the time this book has been published, I would guess that language would have developed even more and some of what I write may already be viewed with suspicion or considered outdated.

There's no way to satisfy everyone with my choice of terms. Personally, I like the openness of LGBTQ+ and the way the plus sign

---

1 People also use "rainbow" to refer to a baby that is conceived and born after a baby was lost to miscarriage. So, a rainbow family could be a queer one, or it could be one that has experienced baby loss, and of course, it could refer to both.

allows for more to be added to the umbrella, and I also like using queer as shorthand, so those are the two terms I will use the most throughout the book.

My aim is to be inclusive, but apologies in advance to anyone who doesn't feel included or who doesn't identify with any of these terms. I hope you will, nonetheless, find something of interest and benefit in the book, even if you don't recognize yourself in the terms I use.

Queer Parenting

My wife and I have two children and I believe they have an advantage in life because they are being raised by LGBTQ+ parents. I know this is a controversial thing to say, so I'll back up a little in order to explain my thinking.

Why Have Kids?

You might wonder why LGBTQ+ people would want to be parents or how we might parent differently. From a basic, evolutionary perspective, well, we feel the same urges to procreate or to parent as non-LGBTQ+ folks.[2] It's a pull, biological in some cases, that some of us feel quite strongly. It doesn't matter to us if we don't have the same equipment as a cisgender, heterosexual couple and if we need to find another route to reproduction; we still long for the experience of raising children.

Some people have told me that if LGBTQ+ people have kids, we're just "aping" heterosexual, cisgender people and being normative in our behavior. Well, I don't see why that's so. LGBTQ+ people have presumably been having children for as long as humans have existed; we might not have called ourselves LGBTQ+ or fully understood our sexuality or gender in the way we do today, but we've been here and queer since the dawn of humanity. What makes parenting something only some people can do? Even if society did consider parenting to generally be the province of non-LGBTQ+ people, why not try to change this and show them how we queers can do it?

Parenting is one of the most challenging, stimulating activities you can do; personally, I've found that it has helped me develop more than anything else I have done or accomplished in my life.

---

2 Yes, I know, not everyone wants to have children and not everyone should have children. If you don't feel the urge to parent, you shouldn't be forced to do so. Here, I'm referring to those of us who genuinely do want children and aren't being pressured into doing so by our families, friends, or societal norms.

Parenting forces you to look at yourself and to face your weaknesses, your insecurities, and your fears; when you're responsible for another life, you have to be less self-focused than you might have previously been, and you need to become the best version of yourself. You probably know this already, but there's no such thing as a perfect person, so don't expect to be a perfect parent or for parenting to perfect you in any way, even if it does change you. Often, you become a slightly different person from who you were before, and this can be a source of pride. Parenting is self-development to the max on a daily basis.

It's also an opportunity to look at your own childhood and to analyze what it was like. For LGBTQ+ people, this may be quite painful if you dealt with homophobia/biphobia/transphobia or abuse, or if you were rejected by relatives. You might realize that how you want to parent is different from how you yourself were parented, and this could entail a certain level of sadness that the child you didn't have such an easy time. Maybe becoming a parent would be a chance for you to make things right in a way, and to get to relive childhood from a different perspective; this could be healing. On the other hand, you might have had a great childhood and you might find you want to use many of the parenting approaches and techniques your own parents did, and this could provoke a new sense of appreciation for your guardians. There might be a combination of things happening for you, so you reject some parenting methods and decide to adopt others. No matter what your experience as a child, becoming a parent yourself allows you to reflect on what your life has been like so far and what you would like it to be in the future.

Having children is a way of contributing to the world (just to be clear, it's definitely not the only way of doing this; you don't have to have children to help make the world a better place). You can raise curious, kind, activist people (or whatever set of adjectives you'd consider important) who can challenge norms and bring broader points of view and help change society for the better for future generations.

Yes, having children is something you can't undo, and for some people, it brings about a sense of loss, such as feeling that they can't work as much as before or party like they used to, or they might worry that their identity has been taken over by the role of being a parent. So, you have to think it through carefully before you start the process. But for many people, even though some days with children can be difficult (indeed, they can be very, very difficult sometimes), in general, you're in for a lot of fun, laughter, surprise, and joy if you have kids. Children can give you another reason to live and can bring more meaning to your life, and that can be enormously fulfilling and enjoyable.

How Many LGBTQ+ People Actually Have Kids?

Some estimates suggest that 1-10% of the population is LGBTQ+; one report suggests that around 4% of people in the U.S. identify as LGBTQ+ (Gates, 2011), while for the UK, around 2.7% of the population identify as LGB (T wasn't included in this study) (Office of National Statistics, 2020). Further research notes that some people don't feel comfortable identifying with those terms—perhaps due to where they live—but do actually behave in ways that would be described as LGBTQ+ (such as having sex/relationships with people of the same sex), and that this implies that the figure is closer to 10% (Spiegelhalter, 2015).

Meanwhile, anywhere from 8-20% of LGBTQ+ people are thought to have children, at least in certain countries (Goldberg & Conron, 2018).[3] As the next chapter discusses, rights vary hugely from country to country, so it isn't necessarily the case that there are loads of LGBTQ+ families in every country in the world. Still, there are some places with quite a lot of children of LGBTQ+ parents. One American study, for example, notes that:

> Between 2 million and 3.7 million children under age 18 have an LGBTQ+ parent. Many of these children

---

3 Interestingly, "same-sex couples with children were far more likely than male/female couples with children to have an adopted child (21.4% versus 3.0%) and/or a foster child (2.9% versus 0.4%)" (Goldberg & Conron, 2018). We'll look more at adoption and fostering below.

are being raised by a single LGBTQ+ parent, or by a different-sex couple where one parent is bisexual. Approximately 191,000 children are being raised by two same-sex parents. Overall, it is estimated that 29% of LGBTQ+ adults are raising a child who is under 18 (Family Equality, 2020).

Similar information from the United Kingdom states:

Figures released by the Office for National Statistics show that in 2019, there were 212,000 same-sex families in the UK, having increased by 40% since 2015. However, the most recent statistics for the number of same-sex couples raising children remain those from 2013, when 12,000 couples were doing so. In March 2015, government statistics for the previous year showed that on average more than 9 children per week were being adopted by LGBT parents, representing 14% of all adoptions (FFLAG, n.d.).

Furthermore, close to 80% of LGBTQ+ people aged 18 to 35 already have or plan on having children (Compton, 2019).

In other words, right now, there are millions of children being raised by LGBTQ+ parents, whether those parents are single, in same-sex relationships, in opposite-sex relationships, in coparenting situations, in poly families, or in other types of families. There are likely to be even more in the coming decades, as more LGBTQ+ people around the world get the right to adopt or access fertility treatment. So, it's important to consider what, if anything, is different about how LGBTQ+ folks parent.

How LGBTQ+ People Parent

As I suggested above, LGBTQ+ people have been parents for as long as there have been people in the world. We might not have been able to parent in our chosen relationship formats or openly as our actual genders and sexualities, but LGBTQ+ people have always been involved in family formation and the raising of children, whether through sexual relationships that perhaps weren't our preferred ones, or as the so-called maiden aunts or bachelor uncles, or in other ways. It is only in recent times that humans have decided that parenting in nuclear families, particularly one-mother, one-father ones, should be the norm, whereas large groupings of relatives and villages would have traditionally been more likely to be involved.

Of course, some people argue that LGBTQ+ folks should not be parents. I don't wish to give their views much space, but one of their worries is that LGBTQ+ parents somehow make children queer them-selves, but of course, this is simply not possible; if parenting worked like that, then many of us who were raised by heterosexual, cisgen-der parents would not be LGBTQ+ ourselves as adults. Furthermore, what would be wrong with having more queer people in the world, if LGBTQ+ parents did influence young people in that way?

Some people are against LGBTQ+ folks generally and feel it is against their god or religious beliefs for LGBTQ+ people to parent, but for those who are believers, why would a god have allowed humans to be LGBTQ+ if that god didn't approve of it? If that god wanted children to have one father and one mother, why would the god allow people to die in childbirth or during their children's childhoods, or allow people to fall out of love and to separate? Why would the god otherwise not make it possible for children to be raised in that particular way? I'm not a theologian, but I have trouble seeing how people can insist that an omnipotent god would want things a particular way, yet not make them that way.

It's hard to combat religious-based anxieties or prejudices here, since, by definition, they are often personal or are shaped by falli-ble religious leaders and by religious texts written by other fallible humans. But other, non-religious concerns about LGBTQ+ parents are starting to be explored in academic research. This research shows that the children of LGBTQ+ parents are not worse off than the children of straight, cisgender parents. When people talk about or conduct research into same-sex or other LGBTQ+ parents, they usually ask if the child of an LGBTQ+ couple is at a disadvantage (Johnson & O'Connor, 2002). Is the child more likely to be bullied? Depressed? Will the child have fewer opportunities in life or be poorer? What social stigma will the child suffer? In fact, the great majority of studies show that "children of gay or lesbian parents fare no worse than other children" (Cornell University Public Policy Research Portal, n.d.). That's useful to know if you're faced with people saying how sorry they feel for the children of LGBTQ+ folks!

Indeed, research suggests that having queer parents isn't a problem in and of itself. What is a problem is that there is stigma and prejudice in the society at large. In other words, if it's a homophobic community or society, then LGBTQ+ people and their families might be looked down upon and might have a more difficult life because of non-LGBTQ+ people's views and how they treat the queers among them (Kuvalanka, Leslie, & Radina, 2013). Anna Fairtlough (2008) researched the children of LGBTQ+ parents and writes:

> What came over most strongly in the young people's accounts was that they identified that the problems they experienced with having a lesbian or gay parent arose almost entirely from other people's negative views about lesbian and gay people (p. 525).

One way to fight and change this is by more LGBTQ+ folks being out and just getting on with living their lives, so more people realize that they know, like, accept, and approve of those who are LGBTQ+. This, in turn, will challenge societal beliefs and lead to more rights and to LGBTQ+ people and families being normalized, and eventually being viewed as, well, kind of boring; some scholars suggest that part of the problem is LGBTQ+ parents being viewed as "different," when it's just about the ways that society sets up hierarchies of sexuality and gender (Hicks, 2005). Of course, we also need to actively fight for our rights, as well as hoping allies might eventually support us. One day, we'll be so visible and accepted that most people will scarcely give us another thought. That's my hope, anyway.

Not only do the children of LGBTQ+ parents seem to have no problematic outcomes when compared to other children, but some research suggests that children raised by LGBTQ+ parents are actually doing better in many ways than those raised by heterosexual, cisgender people. For example, children of LGBTQ+ parents are less likely to play in gender-stereotyped ways, where they believe that certain toys and activities are for one gender while other toys and activities are for another (Goldberg, Kashy, & Smith, 2012). In general, they don't tend to follow traditional gender roles (Stacey & Biblarz, 2001). At home, they don't see fathers doing one thing and mothers doing another, because they don't have a one-father and one-mother set-up, and thus, they don't get taught from a young age that men and women act in distinct ways. So, their play, their activities, and their ways of being are generally not as constricted as they might be if they were raised by heterosexual parents. They won't think, "Dad always makes the money and Mom always cleans the house, so that's how I have to live too." Such children feel less limited and inhibited. What toys and books children have access to, what subjects they feel they can study, and what they see their parents do influences their futures, which means that kids being raised by LGBTQ+ folks have a potentially greater scope for their lives.

In addition, "Teenage boys raised by lesbians are more sexually restrained, less aggressive and more nurturing than boys raised in heterosexual families," while girls raised by LGBTQ+ parents are more adventurous and open about sexuality and sexual experiences (Silsby, 2001). You might be thinking that you don't want sexually adventurous daughters, but I'd personally rather have girls who are confident in their own bodies and their desires than girls who get into bed and allow themselves to be bossed around and treated as objects, simply because they think that's what females should do. Furthermore, research shows that LGBTQ+ couples are better at resolving conflict than heterosexual ones (Gottman et al., 2003). This influences their homelife, which may be more peaceful and less confrontational, and also affects their children, who learn how to "resolve conflict more constructively...and with less animosity" (Caron, 2020).

So why do we see these differences with LGBTQ+ parents? Well, as noted, since we've intentionally become parents, we might be more enthusiastic about this new role. Having kids was a deliberate choice and we realize how lucky we are to live in a time and place that allows us to do so, and that might make us really dote on and appreciate our little ones. We might also be a bit older than non-LGBTQ+ parents, since it can take longer for our adoptions to come through, our fertility treatments to work, or our lives to feel secure enough for children. Being older means we've lived more, have more knowledge of the world, maybe have made more money and feel more financially stable, and perhaps have done our partying and don't mind nights that are sleepless in a whole new way. Frankly, adoption or using a clinic or the purchase of donor sperm from other places is expensive and suggests that such families may have more disposable income or may be more careful at budgeting, and while money certainly isn't everything, it can help sometimes. This isn't necessarily true for everyone, but some of it might be relevant to you.

Many LGBTQ+ people will, unfortunately, have had experiences with bullying, rejection, abuse, and other trauma, and so will make choices about how to parent, where to live, which schools to choose, and so forth that will help our own children feel accepted. Given those tough, painful experiences, we might be more empathetic, which is a key skill in parenting (and in life generally). As LGBTQ+ people, we might also be more likely to live in more liberal, less prejudiced communities, or even to have created intentional communities of our own, since we want to feel welcome and secure, and those sorts of values will inevitably influence our children. We may have gotten rid of the negative, homophobic/ biphobic/transphobic, or otherwise prejudiced people in our lives and have just surrounded ourselves to whatever extent possible with supportive, caring friends and relatives. Being included and accepted will help combat issues such as depression or shame. We will also have some sense of how to help strengthen our children's sense of identity and pride in themselves so that they can both fight back against any prejudice they face, and also be actively anti-racist, anti-phobic, anti-anti-Semitic, and otherwise inclusive. Also, living in neighborhoods filled with diverse types of people and families and going to schools with children who are not identical to them will be educational for our children and help them to learn more about different backgrounds and perspectives, and to be more compassionate towards others.

In general, because LGBTQ+ people don't follow society's explicit or implicit roles for how to live, we feel more able to challenge particular ideas. Considering concepts from a unique perspective and with the freedom that comes from being different is liberating, and that willingness to question and challenge is an excellent trait to teach children. We don't want to raise kids to just do as they're told, or nothing would ever change in society. Showing them that we are true to ourselves and that we live in a way that feels right is a gift that will help them as they get older.

Not all these things are applicable to all LGBTQ+ parents, and some of them assume a certain level of privilege that certainly not all LGBTQ+ people have, but the research does show that there are some distinct advantages for children of LGBTQ+ folks. Still, as I said, it isn't a competition between different types of parents, and we can all learn from one another. However, because so many people critique LGBTQ+ parenting, it can feel helpful to know that there are quite a lot of things in our favor. Even if there weren't, it would still be our right to have children and to parent as we like, but it can be comforting to know that our children do seem to turn out well, and often more than well. That's definitely something to be proud of.

In short, it sounds pretty good to have queer parents! It is both comforting and inspiring to know that children raised by LGBTQ+ people are thriving. In some ways, this is not a surprise, as different families do raise their children differently and that this must lead to some differences in development. LGBTQ+ parents have usually had to carefully think through the decision to become parents and have had to spend more time and money than many cisgender and heterosexual people. I am not implying that non-LGBTQ+ people just thoughtlessly have children because they think they ought to, as although that might be true for some, that isn't the case for all, but certainly, it is a lot harder for some queer people to accidentally get pregnant or to just decide to try for a baby on the spur of the moment. Since LGBTQ+ people have often had to think long and hard about becoming parents and may have had arduous or time-consuming journeys to parenthood, they've also had plenty of time to consider how they might like to parent. Being thoughtful about what you're doing is a good start.

Queering Parenting

I've said that thinking about why you want to be a parent and how you want to parent can lead to LGBTQ+ people raising strong, well-adjusted children who challenge stereotypes. More specifically, how can one queer the idea of parenting or try to parent in a queer way? Based on what academic research around LGBTQ+ parenting suggests, I'd say that we need to start by pondering why we want to become parents and what we liked or didn't like about our own childhoods, before thinking about how to raise the next generation.

We don't have to follow the blueprints set out by our parents, because we're usually already doing things differently from them. Most of us were not raised by queer parents and so, from the outset, we have a distinct difference from our guardians. Andrew Solomon (2012) discusses the difference between what he terms horizontal and vertical identities:

> Because of the transmission of identity from one generation to the next, most children share at least some traits with their parents . . . Attributes and values are passed down from parent to child across the generations not only through strands of DNA, but also through shared cultural norms. Often, however, someone has an inherent or acquired trait that is foreign to his or her parents and must therefore acquire identify from a peer group . . . Such horizontal identities may reflect

recessive genes, random mutations, prenatal influences, or values and preferences that a child does not share with his progenitors (p. 2).

Being LGBTQ+ is frequently a horizontal identity, which gives us the freedom to be ourselves and to follow our own paths, even if that's sometimes scary for us and upsetting to those who raised us.

Our own parents may have been conditioned to have certain beliefs about what a mother did versus what a father did, and they might not have questioned or challenged it (even when they weren't living in norm ways). Even if we have received the same conditioning by society, we often feel less constricted by it for the simple reason that we're not in traditional one-mother, one-father families. We're queer and we can think about our roles in different ways.

So, it's time to consider: Who are you? How do you want to make your family? What kind of parent do you want to be? Why? What can you take from your own childhood and what do you want to discard? What kind of people do you want your children to become? What sort of society do you want to help shape? What are your unique strengths and characteristics and experiences? How can you use them to your advantage when parenting as an LGBTQ+ person?

We don't have to do things in the traditional ways and, often, we can't do them like that, just by dint of who we are and the lives we lead. When we're freed from societal norms, we get a chance to do things on our own terms. As for me, I'm proud to be out and LGBTQ+, and I'm glad my children can see that they have two mothers who make all the decisions for their own lives. That's a thought-provoking lesson in a society that's still patriarchal and misogynist, and I think it's helping my children to become independent, opinionated feminists. I love having a life where I can be myself and parent in a way that I'd call queer.

A Stor, About What Queer Parenting Can Be

H is a queer/bisexual polyamorous woman who produced and raises her son, F, in a coparenting relationship in a cooperative household. She produced F with S, but is not in a romantic relationship with S.

Here, H explains what she thinks is different about queer parenting:

"I do think that LGBTQ+ people relate to children differently. My queer friends have all had adverse childhood experiences that they are still processing. Because of this, there is a deep compassion and respect among us for the emotions and rights of children. Because of our communal way of living, there are people to break F, S, and me out of any damaging dynamic. There have always been people to call me out when I've made arbitrary rules or taken a bad day out on F. Because he was raised that way, he now advocates strongly for himself. We're close to the teenage years now, but I'm not worried that he will feel he has no one to talk to. He has multiple close adults to whom he can complain about his parents and who can then help him work out how to talk to us. I'm almost looking forward to seeing what happens, to be honest!

If you are planning an LGBTQ+ family, I would heartily recommend that you fully open your mind to what a family can look like. Think about friends who might want to be involved and how you can build bonds with them. We started out by cooking together most nights of the week, then living together, then buying a house together, but there are many other ways. Make traditions, live generously, and choose good people. You will find there are many LGBTQ+ adults who do not want children but relish the opportunity to be involved in the life of one. It's a rare privilege to be closely involved but not bear any of the responsibility.

If you are LGBTQ+, it's likely you have had to work towards having a child intentionally. Choose your family that way too and know that your child will benefit from having a bigger community around them as they grow."

The Importance of LGBTQ+ Families Being Visible

Stephanie Wagner, an LGBTQ+ IBCLC who works with many LGBTQ+ families, says it is important for as many of us as possible to be out and visible, because this will help effect societal change. She writes:

"To identify and stand in one's truth when it is anything outside of the heteronormative binary that our society at large is based on, and to affirm one's gender identity and/or sexual orientation, or the absence of, takes strength and courage, and is so powerful and necessary.

To then create a family in that truth of self-identity is even more powerful and necessary for everyone to see and know it is possible. This is how society changes and adapts. This is also how we begin to see more types of families considered normal, and not just the cisgender heteronormative one we regularly see referenced. There is not one definition of what a family is or should be. Far from it! Just as there is not one definition of love. Far from it!

As the LGBTQ+ community expands its outreach, language, presence, and truths, the community, and hopefully, eventually, the rest of society, has no choice but to propel advances in medicine, better laws, and overall understanding and acceptance. By now, most of us have heard the phrase, "Representation Matters," and it *does*. It matters for so many reasons, including in the field of medicine.

LGBTQ+ parents deserve the same awareness, opportunity, and respect as any non-LGBTQ+ parent/family does."

By being ourselves, by living our lives in a way that feels right to us, by not just adhering to the norm, and by insisting that we receive the same rights and treatment that non-LGBTQ+ people do, we can create change in society, not just for ourselves and our children, but for future generations as well. How amazing and powerful is that?

Legal Rights

I live in the United Kingdom, although I grew up in the United States, where this book is being published, so most of the information here is UK- or U.S.-specific. It probably goes without saying that you would need to check what your legal rights are in your country or region before you embark on any family planning. Also, some of what I write here may be outdated by the time the book is published. I'm sorry if you live somewhere that makes it hard for you to be openly LGBTQ+ or to have children, and I hope you find a way forward, perhaps even by being visible or an activist, thereby helping to improve the situation for LGBTQ+ people in your country.

In the UK, the non-profit organization Stonewall lists important dates and facts for LGBTQ+ people on their website (Stonewall, n.d.). In a brief fashion, I will mention a few here that are relevant specifically to parenting. In 2002 in the UK, same-sex couples received the same rights as opposite-sex couples when it comes to adoption. However, it took until 2005 before unmarried couples of any sexuality or gender were allowed to jointly apply for adoption. Single people, also regardless of sexuality or gender, legally can adopt too.

In 2002, same-sex couples were given the right to enter civil partnerships, which were seen as equal to but different from marriage. Arguably, if something is equal but separate, it probably isn't equal. In 2013, same-sex couples were granted the right to full marriage, and this came into force one year later.

In 2008, same-sex parents were given the right to be recognized as legal parents of babies conceived with the use of donor eggs, sperm, or embryos. What this means in practice is, if a same-sex couple is married at the time that a child is conceived, they both can be listed on the birth certificate. They may be required to fill in a form that confirms relevant facts. If they are not married or in a civil partnership and they have conceived with a known donor, the sperm donor may be required to officially give up parental rights, and the non-birth parent will be required to apply to adopt the child.

If this does not happen, that could make the sperm donor liable for child support and the parents might be required to allow access to the child, which may not be a situation you want.

People have the legal right to have their gender confirmed in the UK (Gov-UK, n.d.); the government calls this "acquired" gender, whereas other people prefer to use terms such as "confirmed" or "recognized." Generally, you have to be a legal adult, to have been diagnosed as having gender dysphoria (considered to be a mismatch between your biological sex and your understanding of your own gender), and to have lived as this gender for at least two years with the intention of continuing to do so. What's also useful to know is that this should have no legal impact on your civil partnership or marriage, or on your legal rights as a parent. Some agencies or fertility clinics might not have had experience with trans or non-binary people, but they have no legal footing if they try to discriminate against you.

In terms of fertility treatment, LGBTQ+ individuals and couples have the right to receive fertility treatment. The National Health Service (NHS) in the UK does vary from area to area, so it is best to check what you are entitled to. For example, you may have to prove that you have been trying to get pregnant for six months or a year before you will be allowed to have treatment on the NHS, which obviously may be tricky to show for LGBTQ+ couples. If either person in a couple already has children, the NHS will not provide treatment and you will have to pay privately. In the news recently here in the UK, a lesbian couple has started challenging the discriminatory treatment that LGBTQ+ families face when it comes to NHS-funded fertility treatment (Lawrie, 2021), so perhaps this will change in the near future.

As so often happens in the United States, rights vary from state to state. This is rather depressing, considering that it's thought that around six million Americans have an LGBTQ+ parent, so one would think parental rights should be protected throughout the nation (Gates, 2013). Unfortunately, this lack of consistency means that LGBTQ+ parents may be treated differently depending on where they are located, with, for example, some trans parents being deemed "unfit" and not granted rights or visitation in one county or state, while being trans is (rightfully) regarded as irrelevant in other locations. Similarly, LGBTQ+ people could be eligible for a second-parent adoption in one state but not in another. In the U.S., same-sex marriage was a tumultuous journey, with it being temporarily legal in different times and places, but it finally was recognized as legal across the country in 2015 (American Experience, n.d.). Not long after that, it became legal in every U.S. state for LGBTQ+ people to adopt, whereas previously, it had been piecemeal. However, in some states, there is still no protection against discrimination in the adoption or foster care system.

This means that you may want to consider where in the U.S. you live before you produce children, although I recognize that not everyone has the privilege, the money, the emotional and practical support, and the general wherewithal to move. If you can't move to another state or country, then try to protect yourself as best you can with formal or informal agreements.

In some other countries around the world, it isn't even legal to be LGBTQ+. In still other countries, even if LGBTQ+ people have some rights, LGBTQ+ individuals or couples cannot adopt, marry, get fertility treatment, both (or all) be listed on the birth certificate, and/or identify in any way other than as the gender they were assigned at birth. This can be upsetting and frustrating, and it can also get in the way of family planning. For instance, you may hesitate to use a known sperm donor, if that donor would be given rights in your country that you don't want them to have. So, it may be worth looking into accessing healthcare in another country, if that's an option for you.

If you are in a poly relationship, remember that most countries will not recognize all people as parents (or at least not without a legal battle). So, you may have to decide in advance who will have legal responsibility, and you may choose to write an informal agreement clarifying people's roles, rights, and responsibilities.

Another legal consideration is if you use donated eggs, sperm, or embryos, there may be issues regarding what you are allowed to do with any extra material, such as how long it can be stored and whether you can move it to a different clinic or even a different country.

A Stor, Comparing the U.S. to Europe

Molly, a lesbian, is originally from the U.S. but has lived with her wife in Germany and Austria. They had one child in Germany and are expecting their second in Austria. She writes:

"My son was born in a hospital in Germany. While I've never felt unsafe as an LGBTQ+ person in Germany/Austria, the cultural differences are such that people are not as used to people being open about their sexuality. I found that I was one of the first, if not the first, LGBTQ+ pregnant people that my doctors/midwives were treating. We never felt disrespected but had to clearly introduce ourselves as a married couple and make corrections along the way.

I don't feel we've missed out on any treatment or opportunities because of our family status, but it was legally much more complicated to complete a second-parent adoption from abroad. I will be interested to see how the experience in Austria differs from that of Germany when our daughter is born in the coming weeks, but I'm nearly certain I will not be on her birth certificate after my wife gives birth.

In some ways, I feel more protected in Europe, but in other ways, we are a step behind the LGBTQ+ laws in the U.S., especially as they relate to family planning."

A Stor, Comparing the UK To France

Blanche and Esme are a married French lesbian couple who live in the UK. When they first began thinking about having children, they were living in France, and the laws there influenced their decision-making process. They write:

"Questions of legal parental status have always played an important role in how, as a couple, we imagined building our family. While it may be viewed by some as excessive caution, for us, it was important to limit potential difficulties for us or our children in the future.

Living in France, we could see that same-sex couples were far from acquiring similar rights as heterosexual couples when it comes to family, let alone social acceptance or understanding. Attempts, such as in 2014, in the early stages of the Socialist François Hollande's presidency, to pass progressive family laws, such as medically assisted conception for lesbian couples, were always riddled with obstacles and resistance, resulting in parties backtracking or postponing those projects. We were in our 30s then, and clearly not very optimistic that there would be any such legal framework in place in France in time to protect one of us and our future child.

In France, the non-biological parent, or "social parent," as they are called on official governmental websites—an improvement on the term "biological mother's partner," which is still often used in newspapers—has no legal status and does not appear on the birth certificate.

If and only if both parents are married, the adoption process has been a possible avenue for the non-biological parent since 2013. However, that process is not in any way straight-forward. Until recently, it involved intrusive paperwork such as family statements and supporting photos detailing the involvement of the non-biological parent in the upbringing of the child. It also meant going to court, with the child, to hand those documents in. As a result, even if they go through that process, the non-biological mother is deprived of any parental rights for a substantial amount of time."

A Stor , Comparing the UK to New Zealand

Perse and Deb are a lesbian couple who relocated from the UK to New Zealand. They had already fertilized Deb's eggs in London, and they moved the embryos to New Zealand, but found that laws were somewhat different there. Perse writes:

"Our life as a lesbian couple in Aotearoa New Zealand is lowkey and (thankfully) uneventful. We are one of three lesbian couples (that we know of) raising kids in the town where we live and, while there does not seem to be an LGBTQI+ community locally, we are accepted in our local community without question.

Same-sex marriage was legalized in Aotearoa New Zealand in August 2013, earlier than in the UK, and while urban towns are not teeming with LGBTQI+ people, there are "hot spots" in both Auckland and Wellington, which both hold Pride events each year.

The law surrounding births from donor DNA are quite different here than in the UK. For example, parents using donor DNA have a legal right to access identifying information about the donor from birth, which is not possible in the UK until the child is 18. For us, that meant that the donor we used to create our embryos had to provide permission for our two remaining embryos to be exported to Aotearoa New Zealand, as in the UK, his identity would be kept private until any child born using his DNA turned 18. (Thankfully, he readily gave permission, and we have not sought to access his identifying information).

Another law that was pertinent to our journey to motherhood relates to the fact that donor DNA can normally only be stored for a maximum of ten years. Our donor made his donation in 2012, and our embryos were created in 2016. We transferred the embryos from the UK to Aotearoa New Zealand in 2018, meaning that by the time they arrived, we had a maximum of four years in which to use our remaining embryos before they became at risk of destruction.

Thankfully, Deb became pregnant in late 2018 and, in spite of the intervening global pandemic, became pregnant again in 2020, using our last remaining frozen embryo. (Note: It is possible to extend the 10-year limit, but the donor has to be consulted prior to an extension being granted)."

While the information in this chapter applies specifically to LGBTQ+ couples planning their families together, there is also the issue of what happens when there is separation and/or the blending of families. For example, someone may reproduce with one partner and then separate and bring a new partner into the picture. Or two people who had children separately might bring their families together, and perhaps add further children to the picture. Whether the former partner continues to have contact with and responsibility for the children and whether the new partner takes on a parental role is partially dependent on how the adults and children involved want to shape their relationships and partially on what the law says in their jurisdiction. So, ensure you do your research and know your rights.

Sometimes people think that it feels negative to think about legality. It's perhaps similar to when you're planning to get married and someone brings up the subject of a prenuptial agreement. It can feel wrong, or even like a self-fulfilling prophecy, to talk about divorce when you're planning on a lifetime of blissful couplehood. Yet, it can, in fact, be an enjoyable and useful exercise to discuss what would happen if you split up, because it gives you a chance to think through some issues that you might have otherwise avoided. Discussing the law and your feelings about a range of "what if" scenarios can help you and your partner/s figure out your views about money, where to live, lifestyle preferences, approaches to parenting, sexual needs, politics, religion, involvement with families of origin, and much more. It's easy to assume that you and your partner/s think the same way about things and then it can be a shock to find out that you perhaps differ in your perspective more than you'd realized. Have those conversations early and return to them regularly, since people's opinions and needs change. Consider a discussion about your rights and your hopes an essential part of planning for parenthood.

A Story About Blended Families and Legalities

Above, we met lesbian couple Perse and Deb. Before they got together, Perse was married to a man, with whom she had two children. Here, she writes about how she ensured all three adults and the children were protected in their new familial situation:

"Negotiating parental rights and responsibilities for my older children when I repartnered with (and then subsequently married) Deb was somewhat fraught and definitely time- and resource-consuming.

When Deb moved in with us, we applied for formal parental responsibility for her in relation to the children that, with my ex-husband's consent, was approved by the Family Courts. That meant that the children then had three adults with parental responsibility for them—we could all make decisions about their best interests/welfare, including schooling, housing etc., and any of us were able to agree to necessary medical procedures in case of emergency.

When we decided to emigrate, we needed to ensure the legality of our actions, to prevent any potential future conflict. After discussion and agreement with my children's father that he supported our move to Aotearoa New Zealand as being in the children's best interests—for improved family lifestyle and career opportunities for us as their sole financial providers (my ex-husband was then a full-time student, meaning that he was exempted from paying child maintenance)—I wrote a simple declaratory document that stated the facts: the children's father acknowledged and understood that we would be emigrating to Aotearoa New Zealand, the move was intended to be permanent, and we would continue to honor his parental responsibility until the children became adults.

The document was then provided to a notary, who converted it into appropriate "legalese," had each of us sign it (me, Deb, the children's father), and then legally certified the document, attaching certified copies of the children's birth certificates, Deb's parental responsibility document, and the Family Court Order outlining my full custody rights over the children.

That document gave us the confidence to travel (emigrate) with the children, knowing that their rights and our responsibilities were fully and legally protected, and that we would be able to settle into our new home free of fear of future legal tussles and associated costs.

Making sure that all our plans were fully transparent (i.e., discussed and agreed with the children's father in advance) and that every agreement between the three of us was legally documented was the best investment for a stress-free, trans-global emigration. It allowed us to focus on our move, and to leave behind the adversarial legal entanglements (which is the modus operandi of the British legal system) that had plagued us since I had separated from, and then divorced, my children's father."

No matter where you live, there may be cases where you would want a lawyer involved. This could involve an agreement with a known donor (see Appendix 2) (note that such agreements are usually not legally binding, although they can be helpful) or writing a will or getting parental rights for a stepparent. Again, ensure you know your rights and responsibilities before you start, so you don't end up in a situation that you regret. Check the most up-to-date information for your country or region before you embark on becoming a parent.

Conception: Starting a Famil,

Making a Baby

There are many ways that children can become a part of your life. There's no one right way, and there's no single method that suits every individual or family situation out there. So, have a think about the pros and cons of each before deciding how to proceed. In what follows, I've included some stories from LGBTQ+ people, in which they discuss their choices, so perhaps one or two of those might resonate with you and what you're thinking, or you might feel inspired by how others have done things.

Making a Baby...Separately

There are many reasons why you and your partner/s might have produced children before you got together. Blended families are nothing new (even if some of those "family values" types would like you to believe they are) and they come about in a number of ways.

A common method is for people to have previously been in other opposite-sex or same-sex relationships, and to have produced children in that situation, whether that was through intercourse, fertility treatment, adoption, or any other way. Then, when that relationship ends through separation, divorce, death, or willingly uncoupling, one or more of the partners might find themselves in a new relationship. I would guess that before we LGBTQ+ people had as much visibility and as many legal rights as we do now in many countries, many of us would have felt pressured to be in opposite-sex relationships and would thus have reproduced like that. Then, when we felt safer and more comfortable coming out, we found queer relationships that worked better for us, and we brought our children into them.

It is also possible that people have produced children on their own or in other arrangements, such as coparenting or a cooperative. They may have mixed sperm from one friend with an egg from another, knowingly choosing to reproduce together, despite not wanting or needing a more permanent situation.

Regardless of how the child was made, moving on from one situation to another might bring about a constellation of new familial connections, and people might use terms such as stepparent/stepmother/stepfather, stepsibling/stepsister/stepbrother, aunt/uncle, sister/brother, cousin, and so on. There is a lot of flexibility in how people might relate to one another, and of course, there could be tensions, as well as love and good times.

Pros and Cons of Making A Baby Separately

PROS	CONS
You might have enjoyed your relationship and experiences in your previous situation and retain good memories.	You may be sad to have missed out on producing children together with your current partner/s.
You may have had the access to the rights and technologies needed to make children in your previous situation.	You may not have the access to the rights and technologies needed to make children in your current situation.
You can challenge ideas about what families look like and how families are made.	Blending families can be challenging at times.
You can experience different relationships and situations.	You may have to retain contact with coparents or exes that you would rather not have contact with.

A Stor, from Someone Who Stepparented

Max, a lesbian, became a parent when she moved in with a partner who had children. The children were aged 8 and 11. Max writes:

"My partner and her former husband had an amicable divorce. They were both happy to be moving on with their lives and I got on with him pretty well. Things worked out fine initially, with the children splitting their time between their dad's house and the house where their mum and I lived.

I threw myself into being a stepparent and probably made the mistake of not setting boundaries and ensuring that I had time to myself, but that would have just seemed selfish. I didn't have any legal rights around them, but I was doing everything for them, especially because their mother had bouts of mental health difficulties, sometimes severe ones, which meant I was the responsible adult some of the time (often in crisis situations).

When their dad got more serious about a new woman and moved in with her, giving up his flat, it got difficult because she didn't really like children. Their father was influenced by this and stopped having the children when he was supposed to, and when the children realized they weren't so welcome there, they were less and less keen to go.

This was tough for the kids, because their father was now flaky and not being the dad he had been, but it was also tough for me, because I never got the breaks from parenting that by then I realized I needed. I'd think I was going to have a weekend off from caring for everyone, and then it wouldn't happen, and the kids would be upset about the way their father had cancelled on them again. There was never any respite.

After some years, this all took a toll on me and ultimately, I had to protect my own mental health. I split up with their mother (there were other issues as well) and while I had visits with the children for a while, this was awkward, and it dwindled. I'd been their stepmother and main carer for all that time, and in the end, I had no relationship with them.

Looking back, I'd say I should have made more space for myself, so I didn't feel so overwhelmed by everything. I don't think that would have saved the relationship, but it would have made it easier to think through things and properly assess the situation as it changed. "

A Stor, About Blending and Extending a Famil,

As mentioned earlier, Perse is a lesbian who was previously married to a man and had two children with him. After her divorce, she met Deb, also a lesbian.

Perse explains how it worked when Deb joined their family:

"When Deb moved in with my kids and me, they were 11 and 10 years old, and I had been separated from their father for four years and divorced for a year.

My son (then 10 years old) certainly found the transition to me re-partnering, and re-partnering with a woman, far easier than my daughter (then almost 12 years old), who seemed afraid of losing me.

Deb never attempted to be anything other than another adult in the house (i.e., not a second parent), and my partner, and she waited for time to show the children that she was a permanent fixture and not a threat to their relationship with me.

She got involved in the practical aspects of rearing children—making sure that the things they needed for their packed lunches were on the shopping list, helping them get organized for school, driving them to sports fixtures—and she joined us on all our weekend family outings. She and I shared the cooking and housework chores so that right from the start, the kids saw us working together to care for them, but she left the emotional and disciplinary aspects of mothering my kids to me. By doing that, she naturally navigated what could have been a difficult period for us as a family and gave the kids space to accept her into their lives without pressure (which prevented drama).

When we realized that my daughter was struggling, Deb willingly offered to take my son out for the day so that I could spend some time alone with her and reassure her that Deb's presence in our lives would not rob us of our close bond.

Ultimately, Deb is a hugely pragmatic woman, who is emotionally stable and has great self-esteem, and she knew that she didn't need to win my kids over. She knew and accepted that her presence in their lives was not of their choosing, and she intuitively understood that demonstrating her commitment to us all, over time, would offer the best opportunity for her to be accepted into our family.

The kids quickly learned that they could rely on Deb to be there for them, to help provide for them, to care for them, and also to be there for me. Having a partner with whom to share the load of raising kids helped me become a better mother, which the kids noticed too. They saw my stress levels rapidly decline and my workload lighten as Deb took some of the strain and they saw me begin to have some leisure time that allowed me to take up hobbies, which exponentially improved my mental health. As a result of Deb's additional income, we were able to go on holiday for the first time in a long time, which began the process of building new family memories.

Deb then got pregnant. By the time the first of the two younger children were born, the older kids were 15 and 14 years old, and Deb and I had been together for four years. We had already been through a lot—we had gotten married, created a successful blended family, moved across the world from the UK to Aotearoa New Zealand, lived through a miscarriage, and moved house three times, and then we extended our family by first one, and then two new children.

The older kids are absolutely besotted with the little ones, and there is no room in anyone's minds (let alone hearts) for any argument that our lack of blood ties—the little ones are not biologically related to me or the older kids—undermines our fierce and unwavering love for each other.

Until I met Deb, I knew that I wouldn't have any more children. In fact, I made that clear to her when we first got together! However, having the privilege to meet and marry someone as loving, committed, dependable, and generous as Deb made having more kids not only a possibility, but an active desire.

Deb is a natural when it comes to parenting, and it has been wonderful to see her blossom into the most loving and engaged primary mother to the little two. The older kids are fantastic with the younger ones, and our older daughter has decided to defer her university placement to give her another year with the babies before she goes away. It is amazing to see the teens step up as role models to the younger ones, and to start to practice their own parenting skills—putting boundaries round the younger ones' behavior, risk assessing and keeping them safe, listening to them, supporting their play and development, and encouraging their inquisitiveness. I could not be prouder of the blended and extended family we have become."

Making a Baby Together (Or on Your Own)

So, you've gotten together with a partner or partners or you're ready to do this thing on your own. You've decided that your life would probably be better with a child in it. What should you think about next?

Some Questions to Consider

Why is now the right time for parenting?
What method/s do I want to use to become a parent and why?
Am I physically, mentally, and emotionally healthy and ready?
Do I have the money necessary to become a parent through the more expensive routes?
Do I have support around me, whether from partner/s, relatives, friends, employers, and community?
What sort of parent do I want to be and why?
Does anyone want to physically experience pregnancy, or should we become parents in another way?
Where will the sperm, the egg, and the uterus come from in order to make a baby?
If I am partnered, which partner is going to get pregnant and how will the other partner/s feel about this?
How will we handle it if one of us wants to get pregnant but cannot?
If there are two or more of us with a uterus who want to be pregnant, would we want to get pregnant at the same time or in close consecutive order or at different stages? How would this work, practically speaking?
Will I experience gender dysphoria if I get pregnant and/or breastfeed or chestfeed? What support do I have for dealing with this?

| How much will my family of origin be involved and in what ways? |
| How will be the legal arrangements around parental responsibility? |
| How might parenting affect my relationships with my partner/s and other people? |
| How will we manage issues such as parental leave, childcare, and work? |

Once you've had some time to think through issues such as these, you will begin to have a sense of how exactly you want to make the journey to parenthood.

Fostering and Adoption

Fostering and adoption are ways to make or increase your family without having to go through conception, pregnancy, and birth. Fostering or adopting may also feel right to you if you are concerned about overpopulation and the environmental impact of producing children, or if you worry about all the children out there who need homes. You may choose to foster or adopt relatives whose parents cannot care for them. You can foster and/or adopt, and also have biological children if that seems best for you.

Fostering means taking in a child on a temporary basis, although this could range from short-term to long-term, and could eventually lead to permanence. The child might be having a tough time at home, or they might be moving between placements, or their parents or carers might need some emergency respite. You might start fostering someone and go on to adopt them. To foster, you generally need to go through an assessment, which may include a home visit, references from friends or employers, in-depth discussions, and more. Your gender or sexuality should not play any role, though obviously this does vary by country, and subconscious bias can influence how an individual or agency interacts with you. You will probably be required to have a separate bedroom for the child. In a fostering situation, you will often also have to attend meetings with social workers, teachers, or others involved in the child's life, and you may well be expected to go through training. You may need to facilitate meetings between the child and their biological family. Depending on the situation and where you live, you might receive a foster carer's allowance to help defray the costs of raising the child, or there may be other forms of support, such as activities or services.

Adoptions have to happen through adoption agencies. As with fostering, you will go through an assessment, which can be more or less in-depth, and you will be expected to provide references and evidence that you are safe to be with children, and to possibly undergo a medical evaluation. All this can feel intrusive but is meant to ensure the safety of the children. Additionally, there can be extensive costs, depending on your agency and what they charge for.

Whether you foster or adopt, you are most likely to have no biological connection to the child (unless you can foster or adopt a relative, which does happen sometimes). Having a biological connection matters to some people but is less important to others. It is important that you think through how you feel about it. Most of us LGBTQ+ people know that love makes a family, given how some of us have been rejected or mistreated by our families of origin, but despite that, the biological urge to procreate can be strong for some.

It is also useful to consider how prepared you feel for living with and caring for a child who may have experienced a difficult upbringing. If someone needs fostering or adoption, it is because their parents were unable or unwilling to raise them, and the child will have thoughts and feelings about this and about their family of origin. You may need to support someone who feels rejected, who has experienced or witnessed abuse, is upset or confused about what has happened in their life, and/or has disabilities. Fostered or adopted children may also later want information about their families of origin, which you may or may not be able to provide.

You will have to consider how permanent you want the situation to be; fostering can be long-term, but adoption definitely is. You may prefer getting to know a range of children over time, as in fostering. It is also possible to create a home with people from a variety of genders, ethnicities, abilities, and religions, which may be something that is important to you.

In short, if you want to give a child a loving, safe home, and if having a child is more of a concern than giving birth to one, then fostering and/or adopting may be the best choice for you.

Pros and Cons of Fostering and Adoption

PROS	CONS
You don't have to get pregnant or give birth.	Adoption can be expensive. You may also be required to have a spare room, which may demand that you move to a larger home.
You will be helping someone who already exists and needs support, and you will also be helping their family of origin.	You will likely not have a biological connection to the child (unless they are a relative).
You want to take care of an older child, not a baby (though some babies are available).	You will have to go through an assessment, which can feel intrusive.
You will not be contributing to overpopulation or environmental issues by producing more children.	You may be rejected as a foster carer or as an adoptive parent, although you can challenge this decision.
You could be entitled to adoption leave and you may get financial support if you foster.	You may have to provide a higher level of emotional or physical support to the child than you expected, although you will be entitled to training and other help.

A Stor from Someone Who Plans to Foster

Emily Karp describes herself as a "cis woman who is gray-aromantic, pan-alterous (I might date someone of any gender and feel alterous feelings for any possible gender of person), and kissing-averse and sex-averse asexual." She is a cofounder of The Ace and Aro Advocacy Project.

Emily describes her relationship in this way:

"We are deeply bonded in a way where neither she nor I desire anything sexual, nor even kissing, hand-holding, or cuddling. We're happy with being like super close friends in a committed partnership with intentions to get married and buy a house together one day and before all that, live together, and in about four years, start working towards becoming parents. Together."

Their plans to have children include possibly using a male relative of Emily's as a known donor and definitely to foster. This is what Emily writes about her desire to foster:

"It's been such a dream of mine for so long to foster children, ever since I was 13 years old and growing up with my abusive mom, and knowing I was still lucky to have my dad and certain other adults in my life. I wanted to be able to foster and/or adopt an older child ever since, and the desire has only grown stronger over the years. My current partner and I both wish to prioritize being a trauma-informed and educated foster parent who prioritizes what's best for any foster youth in our home and prioritizes reunification if that's what's best, only seeing adoption as a last resort that we would be happy to step up and do if the kid(s) needed us to.

I joined many Facebook groups and YouTube channels and read blogs, etc. from adult adoptees and former foster youth, and I strongly believe domestic infant adoption is unethical the way it is currently practiced in the USA. Also, a lot of foster parents are unethically approaching foster care as a way to adopt instead of what it so often really is: a temporary guardianship prior to kids being reunified with their parents. But it seems, ultimately, like the U.S. foster care system desperately needs more foster parents willing to approach traumatized kids with compassion and wisdom, and also be sympathetic to their parents and I really want to be that kind of person for foster kids. I was so excited to meet my current partner and realize she felt so similarly about all of it. She had such similar foster care dreams as me.

I do wonder if part of what made me so heavily consider foster care, in addition to my own history in my childhood with my abusive mother, and pop culture narratives I consumed through television and novels as well, was deep down knowing I was a pan-alterous, gray-aromantic, sex-averse asexual. I wonder if knowing I wanted to foster and/or adopt more than have a baby of my own was always tied in some intrinsic way to my sex-aversion.

I'm worried a little about homophobic discrimination when it comes to being in a same-gender partnership when we one day go through a foster care system."

A Stor, from Someone Who Adopted

Christina and her partner, both lesbians, adopted three children. Christina writes:

"We fostered to adopt. Adoption is something I've always wanted to do. There are too many kids that don't have families.

For the most part, we were treated well. We were not chosen for some kids because caseworkers felt kids needed a male figure. Some bio parents were unkind to us.

We have adopted three amazing kiddos. We've also had the pleasure of fostering many other kids that have made a difference in our lives."

Another Stor, from Someone Who Adopted

Eric and his husband, both gay men, adopted their son. He explains what made them choose to adopt and he gives some advice on going through the process:

"We decided to adopt after I went through an intensive therapy program to help me resolve a lifetime of PTSD due to growing up in a violent household. I had a closeted father, who really didn't want to be married to a woman, and an alcoholic mother who drank because her arrangement didn't turn out the way she thought it would. I also experienced extreme bullying because I was gay.

I wanted to help one or two kids have a better life and resolve their trauma while they were still children, instead of having to wait well into their adult years like I did. We set out with the goal to specifically help those LGBT+ kids in foster care kicked out of their homes solely because of their sexual orientation. We had read many articles stating that up to 40% of kids in foster care are there simply because they came out to their parents and were ejected from their homes.

However, I was told by a case worker, upon us inquiring if there were any LGBT+ kids that they knew of who were up for adoption, that no agency across the country will readily and openly identify any child as such (with the exception of transgender children, since it is impossible to hide that) and that we, as a same-sex couple, might come under scrutiny or even be blacklisted for trying to adopt a self-identified LGBT+ child. They said it has become accepted for same-sex couples to adopt straight children, and it is acceptable for straight couples to adopt LGBT+ kids, and it is acceptable for single people to adopt any kids, and it is acceptable for people to adopt children that are a different race but it is not accepted that the best place for a LGBT+ child is with an LGBT+ couple. I guess the world fears that they will somehow be made more gay or indoctrinated. I have no words for this.

Even though we reside in a Southern Bible Belt state in the U.S., I was shocked that through the whole process, we were treated with respect, just like any other married couple, when dealing with anyone in the state foster care system (we decided to complete the foster parent/adoptive parent process through the state, not through a private agency). We have not detected any discrimination or pushback from any state worker at any point in this process.

We adopted one boy, who came to us at 8 years old and is now almost 11, and we are making it work. It was rough in the beginning.

There were two times when we put in the 14-day notice to surrender him but then changed our minds (after the case workers agreed to allowing more services to support him, which I found out through other local foster parents that he should have been receiving from day one of being placed with us).

There are some things I would like to share about the whole process. First, and most important: everyone working in the system lies a lot about everything. The descriptions or details we were given about kids available for adoption (or the details you see on any of the state adoption websites such as "meet the children") are far from the truth. Always ask questions, multiple times and in different ways, to try to get to the truth.

Don't be afraid to ask questions of the children either, since they are receiving lies on their end as well. In our case, we received a call about a boy that was up for adoption and needed a placement quickly since he was unexpectedly pulled from his current adoptive placement. We were told that this boy had a high likelihood of being gay in the future because of some of his current/past behaviors. We were also told that the boy said he would be okay with two dads. We were only given two hours to decide and also told that an opportunity like this rarely comes around (since the system doesn't openly acknowledge the existence of LGBT+ kids). We decided to take him in.

Two weeks into the placement, he spotted our wedding photo and asked me if we were married. I told him yes, then asked him if he had been told that before we met him. He said no, then screamed out, "I hate gay people," ran to his room, locked the door, and continued to scream at the top of his lungs. This is the same boy that we ended up adopting (after lots of therapy sessions for him).

We wonder if having two dads is going to cause him more trauma. He tells us about kids he becomes friends with in school, but eventually, those kids' parents don't seem to let their child come over to play with our son or invite him over to play at their house. A recent comment a girl made to our son sums it up. He said a girl in his class told him, "Your dads are going to turn you gay." I occasionally also hear him being asked, "Where is your mom?"

Any same-sex couple needs to consider the difficulties that the child will experience and be prepared to counter-balance that with positive experiences so that they won't become isolated from other children, and then they might blame you for that instead of the closed-mindedness of the other parents."

Another Story from Someone Who Adopted

Julie, a lesbian, and her partner adopted. Here, Julie describes their experience:

"Adoption was always something I was aware of as my childhood friend was adopted and my auntie and cousins had been foster carers, so I never saw adoption as a plan B. We are both socially minded too so it meant that we could have a family by helping a child or children. Genetics have never been important to us.

The adoption process for us took 19 months from us attending an open evening to our little boy moving into his forever home. These 19 months consisted of many things, such as filling in paperwork and a social worker coming to chat to us once a week for a couple of months. The social worker then writes a report on you and this report is put forward to a panel who then approve you as prospective adopters.

Once you are approved, you then work with your social worker to get matched with a child. In our case, we were approved for one child up to the age of 2 years old. We attended profiling events, fun days where some children were present, and we also looked at paper profiles.

We found our son via a paper profile that our social worker had emailed to us. Once we read his backstory and saw his face, we knew, and we were smitten.

Our social worker arranged a "bump into" at his foster carer's house. This was an opportunity to meet him and ask the foster carer any questions. This meeting was an absolute mix of emotions, as it's still not set in stone, so you try not to get too carried away but at the same time, this is the first time you're meeting your child. He was napping when we first got there and then the foster carer went to get him and at the time he still wasn't walking. She put him on the floor with some toys and after a short while he held on to the fire guard and shuffled along to me.

After a few further meetings with social workers, we were officially linked, and this was agreed by a panel.

Once your child moves in, you have shared parental authority with the local authority. It took a further nine months for our case to go to court and for the adoption order to be granted.

Around four months after our little boy came home, we found out that he was to become a big brother, so the process started again for us, as we were approached by social services to see if we would also care for the baby. This was an immediate yes, as we are passionate about trying to keep siblings together.

The process the second time round was slightly different, as they just needed to update our information, but the biggest difference was, as the baby was unborn, we were getting assessed for an early permanence placement also known as foster-to-adopt. Adoption is always a last resort so before we could officially adopt the baby, the birth family had to be considered and assessed.

After assessments of the birth family had been done, the case went to court and the placement then switched to adoption but again with shared parental responsibility with the local authority. This then goes back to court to become a full adoption.

Although adoption is a longer process, we don't regret any of it. There can be many difficult decisions to make as adoption has varying levels of trauma since the majority of children have been removed from their birth family rather than relinquished. We had to do a lot of reading and training in the process, and this prepares you for how to deal with different situations.

We speak openly to our children about different types of families, and this includes how some families have moms and dads and some have two moms, and some children live with birth families and some children are adopted. Everything is discussed in age-appropriate ways, and we often use books so the children can understand."

Biological Children

If you want to have a biological child and you have no known medical issues that prevent this from happening, you then need to decide how to go about getting sperm to meet an egg and to grow in a uterus. From a practical point of view, you also need to think about where and how you want to make the baby, and how much money and time you'll spend on it before potentially trying a different method.

In short, you need to figure out these things: Whose egg? Whose sperm? Whose uterus? If multiple children are planned, will the sperm and eggs come from the same source or different ones? Is this going to happen at home or in a medical facility? Will intercourse or insemination be involved? In which region/country will this take place and how will that affect everyone's rights? How much money will be spent on the process? How much time will be devoted to it? What will happen if this doesn't work?

From a long-term point of view, there are even more questions. Some were already mentioned earlier in this chapter and in the section on legal rights, but to sum them up: Who will be the parent/s or guardian/s and how might that affect their relationship? How might people feel if their biological material isn't used but they are involved in caring for the child? How will they feel if they aren't considered a parent, but some biological material came from them? Who is financially responsible and how does that relate to contact with the child? What will happen if a guardian dies? These sorts of things are hard to predict, of course, but it is usually worth talking them over in advance, nevertheless.

For now, though, let's focus on the practical stuff. You may have the egg, sperm, and uterus within your relationship already, but if not, you need to look to donation. There are two types: known and unknown.

Known Donor

A known donor is just what it sounds like: a donor who is known to you and possibly also to your child. Most often, this refers to a sperm donor, but you can also have known egg donors. People who donate an egg or some sperm are usually called donors, but in some cases, they are a bigger part of the child's life and might even be given a parental title. It is also important to differentiate between donors who are known to you from conception and donors whose information children can access when they are eighteen. This section refers to the former, as the latter is often called unknown (as they aren't known from conception, even if they can be known later).

Often, people choose known donors because they want access to biological information that may affect the child's health or who the child turns out to be, or because they want to have a relationship with the donor, or because they want both information and a relationship. While many fertility clinics or sperm banks provide a certain level of information about the donor, it is frequently limited, or at least it is until the child turns 18 and can legally request more data. For some people, it feels important to have more.

Known donors might be friends, relatives, or ex-partners, or they can be people you have found on websites or social media dedicated to connecting potential donors with potential parents. Where you met your donor may influence how much you know about them and what sort of relationship you may have in the future.

If a sperm or egg donor is a relative, that can also increase the connection that the parents have with the child. For example, in a two-mother family, the brother or cousin of one mother may donate sperm that is used to fertilize the egg of the other mother. That way, both mothers are genetically related to the child, which is something that matters to some people.

Having a donor who is a friend or relative may also mean that that person will play a role in the child's life. It could be that they are known as a family friend, or you may prefer to give them a title such as Mom/Dad or Aunt/Uncle. Some children have regular overnight stays with donors or go on trips with them, while others might only see them once a year, if that. The amount and type of contact could vary over the years, as circumstances change. Some people, for instance, are more comfortable hanging out with older children rather than babies, or you may move closer or further to the donor because of your job. Not all donors see the children they helped make, however. Some have their own families to prioritize, or are not interested, or have other reasons for wanting to keep their distance. Not all children want to have a relationship with their donor.

If the people involved have the relevant body parts and want to have sex to create a baby, that is an option. I don't really need to give you any more information on that other than to say have fun and good luck! If you don't have the parts and/or don't want to have sex, or if there are fertility issues, then insemination is most likely the way forward.

A man or trans woman can donate sperm either at home or at a clinic. Whatever the location, it simply requires them to masturbate and catch the sperm in an appropriate container (I am aware that this isn't quite as easy as I made it sound). Being at home requires that the person inseminating keep track of their menstrual cycle and try to time donation so that it happens while they are ovulating (see Appendix 1 for an ovulation chart; you can also use an app). If possible, you may wish to spend a few days together, so the sperm donor can produce a few lots of sperm so you can attempt several inseminations, just as an opposite-sex couple would aim to have intercourse multiple times during the period of ovulation. The downside with doing this at home (or in a hotel, or any other appropriate location) is that you may feel awkward about masturbating with others aware of what you are doing or about the sperm handover. In addition, you will likely not have any evidence about the donor's health, including their sexual health, so you would have to take it on trust that they have no illnesses.

On the other hand, if you go to a clinic, you will be required to pay for a variety of tests on the known donor and possibly on their sperm as well. You may also be required to undergo counseling, separately and/or together, to show evidence of knowing what exactly you are getting into—a requirement that people making babies in the traditional way need not meet. Furthermore, you may be expected to pay storage fees for the sperm, especially if you hope to use it to make two or more children. Some people find a clinic, well, clinical and not at all conducive to producing sperm, whereas others may prefer the detached nature of donating there. If a clinic is involved, fertilization and insemination will also take place there, which again adds increased costs. Depending on where you live, you may have to travel some distance to get to the clinic.

If you are an individual or a couple/family without an egg—whether because you are a man (or two or more men) or because you are not able or willing to use your own eggs—then you could have an anonymous donor through a clinic or you can ask a friend or relative for an egg. If it is a friend or relative who is serving as an egg donor, they will generally need to undergo testing at a fertility clinic and/or a doctor's office and they will have to take medications to stimulate their follicle growth. In other words, this process is harder on the egg donor's body than on the sperm donor's body and does involve the use of hormones, as well as multiple ultrasounds and other intrusive treatments, including egg collection.

You may also choose to be a donor yourself, either as the sperm donor or an egg donor. If you have plenty of eggs yourself, you might choose to share them with others, which could decrease your own costs if you need to pay for fertility treatment. If you want to share sperm, you may get some payment for it, but generally, this does not decrease your costs for fertility treatment. However, if you share sperm informally, you sometimes can get expenses paid for.

There are websites and social media groups for people to try to meet and connect with potential known donors. There have been stories about men trying to use these sites to meet women to have sex with, but there have also been success stories, where people have found a donor they liked and made a friend for life. No matter how you meet a potential donor, you will want to spend quite a bit of time talking to them about what donating means and what your relationship might look like in the future, if a child were to result.

See Appendix 2 for suggested topics to include in a contract with a known donor. Remember that it is not legally binding, but it can be helpful to have discussions about these issues and to sign a contract to show your intentions. If you later find that you have disagreements about your situation, you can return to your contract, perhaps during a session with a counsellor or family therapist.

Pros and Cons of a Known Donor

PROS	CONS
You get access to biological information from the donor.	Getting sperm can be awkward/funny.
You may already have or could develop a relationship with the donor.	You may find that the donor wishes to be involved more or less than you/they had anticipated.
You know where the biological material came from.	You may be stuck having contact with someone who you later realize you don't wish to be stuck with.
Your child may like knowing the donor or the donor's family.	Your child may not want a relationship with the donor, which could be awkward or could impact your relationship with the donor.

A Story from a Known Sperm Donor

Fred, a straight cis man, agreed to donate sperm to a couple comprising a lesbian and a trans man. Fred says:

"I chose to donate because I believe that raising children with loving parents is what's most important. LGBTQ couples have a unique journey that any child can benefit from being a part of. All loving and capable couples deserve the right to have a family. Saying yes felt right to me and aligned with the values I hold dear."

A Story from Someone Who Chose a Known Donor

Molly, a lesbian, and her wife wavered between using a known donor or an unknown one. Molly writes:

"We have a 4-year-old son and are expecting our second baby in just two weeks. Both were conceived with a known donor, one of my best friends from college. While we were lucky and conceived both kids fairly easily, the decision on how to have children was fairly long and somewhat tortured. I knew lots of people in our position who went to a sperm bank. We looked into several, even purchasing access to donor profiles, etc., but I couldn't shake a kind of icky feeling about the process.

The oddness of shopping for sperm based on characteristics, the number of children that could be born from one donor, and the detached language used to describe the material were off-putting to me. We decided to ask to speak to nearly every queer couple we knew who had kids to try and normalize things, but it only put me off more. I heard so many people say, "Biology doesn't matter at all; it's just sperm; we only needed this one thing from that person, we don't really care who he is."

I came to realize that those things were not true for me, even if they were for other people. Biology does matter to me; it's not "just sperm," or some disembodied product used to make a baby. With a lot of self-reflection (and therapy) I came to understand what may be the root of these feelings for me. I am the descendent of a splintered family tree, including a Polish Jewish Holocaust survivor (my maternal grandfather) who I never met and whose siblings were scattered across the world after escaping Poland, which meant I lacked a true sense of rootedness in my identity and family lineage, since I did not have access to a part of that lineage. These were all things I wanted to avoid passing down to the children my wife and I were planning to create, so leaving a big question mark where their other genetic parent should be wasn't something I wanted to do.

Finally, I went to dinner with a friend who had a child with her partner with the help of a friend and known donor. Everything she said clicked for me and I finally found my comfort and confidence to go this route. We were lucky that C, a dear friend of mine from college, agreed to help us right away. We were cautious at first to keep boundaries, referring to him as the "donor," rather than "father" or any form thereof, and with the physical distance between us (C in New York and us in Europe), we had complete autonomy as parents.

I've since evolved a lot on that stance, though, and think of C fully as the father of my children. He does not play the social role of a father/dad, but he is responsible for half of the genes that make up so much of who they are. We tend to use the term "bio dad" when referring to him.

He and our son have met three times, and this last meeting was very special. It had been so long due to the pandemic and distance, but our son was also at such an age that he was much more interested and interactive with his bio dad. While he knows in factual terms who C is to him, I'm not sure that he fully grasps what that means at this age. Yet, he's completely drawn to C in a way that he isn't to other people he doesn't know well, especially men. I love seeing their connection and hope that we can live closer in the future so that it's a more regular thing."

A Stor, from Someone Who Used
Two Different Known Donors

Heather, a queer cis woman, and her husband Mitch, a trans man, have two children. The children have two different known donors. Heather explains:

"Shortly after our first son turned 1, I became convinced I needed another baby. My husband Mitch, terrified of more sleepless nights, wasn't convinced but soon became excited about the prospect.

For our first child, we'd used my friend Chris for our donor, getting pregnant via home insemination. Chris became known as Poppy, someone special, but not a parent. He lived in San Francisco with his husband David, and we only saw him once or twice a year.

I assumed we would use him for a donor again, but my husband had a different idea. He wanted to use David. My husband liked that David's ancestry and physical appearance were more similar to him. The most important part of this suggestion for Mitch was that he thought it would bring the four of us closer together, tying strings between all of us in a unique way.

Initially, I was more worried than excited, running through all the reasons this could be a bad idea: What if Chris wanted to be Involved but David didn't? What if they got divorced and David disappeared from the picture? What if one died? How might each of these scenarios create a wedge between our son and his future sibling?

But the more we talked, the more I realized that most of these fears were rooted in traditional ideas about biology and family concepts that we were already breaking down and redefining. I liked and respected David and how he moved through the world and the fact was he was already a part of our child's life. Of course, we still had to run this by David and Chris, as clearly it wasn't our decision alone to make in the first place.

After his own initial hesitation and questions, David agreed. We got pregnant at home again, but this time shipping sperm across country. David became Pippy. So, we have Pippy and Poppy. Although life and the pandemic have prevented us from seeing each other as often as we'd like, they are a deep and important part of our life, and we wouldn't have done this any other way."

Unknown Donor

In this section, I am referring to two types of unknown donor. The first type is not so common now, but in earlier times, if someone needed to buy sperm or eggs, they were often given few or no options, received minimal information about the donor, and were never given the chance to get more details later. At the time, when this was usually relevant to heterosexual families, this was thought to be the better approach. People were more secretive about egg or sperm donation and thought it shameful, so doctors even recommended that parents not tell children about their conception. As Tabitha Freeman et al. (2016) note:

> Historically, rates of disclosure in families headed by heterosexual couple families have been very low, with most parents deciding against telling their children about their donor origins (p. 593).

A one-mother, one-father family could pretend that they did not use donation and children would not necessarily find out that the eggs or sperm came from different sources than they believed (although, if they did find out later, they might be unhappy about not having been told the truth (see Kleeman, 2021)).

These days, the approach of hiding the truth or lying is no longer common, especially in Western countries, and in any case, it wouldn't work in most LGBTQ+ families. The situation for LGBTQ+ parents is different from that of cisgender, heterosexual parents, in that children will eventually gain a basic understanding of biology and reproduction, and will figure out that their two mothers or two fathers (or other possible family set-ups) most likely could not have made the children easily, without some sort of donation.

The second type of unknown donor is one that could be more appropriately called unknown-now-possibly-known-later. This is where someone has donated sperm or eggs to a sperm bank or fertility clinic and the people purchasing the sperm or eggs can access some basic information about the donor. The conceived child generally is allowed to get more information about and even contact details for their donor when they turn eighteen. At that stage, the unknown donor might become a known one, even if the child just knows about them rather than knowing them in person.

Donations in this category are always formal, since you don't know the donor, and that also means they cost more than informal donations, but you do have the comfort of knowing you don't just have to go on trust. If there is anything medically wrong with the sperm or eggs, this will be flagged up by the clinic or sperm bank.

When you have decided to purchase donor sperm or eggs, you can either choose an option offered by your clinic or, in the case of sperm, you can order it from elsewhere and have it sent to your clinic. If you decide to go with what the fertility clinic has, you may be asked about a few key features you would like (such as hair or eye color or ethnicity, so that some features match you and/or your partner). But then again, you may not get a choice, because of a limited array of options, such as if you are using a donor embryo (where the egg and sperm have already met). If you do get a choice at your clinic, they will offer you a few suggestions and you can take it from there.

If you decide to use a sperm bank, you will be able to access hundreds of profiles, sometimes only after you pay a fee. This can be thrilling or positively dizzying. You will need to narrow it down somehow—whether by the donor's baby pictures or by their career or their religion, or any of many other possible characteristics. You might find this enjoyable to do over a glass, or a bottle, of wine, or you might feel overwhelmed. Some people have told me they literally just pointed at the first one they saw and took it, whereas others spent months choosing. If you do buy it from a source like this, you will need to coordinate shipment from your bank to your clinic (or to your house, if you're inseminating at home), and then the clinic will store the material until you need it. You may also find that the first donor you choose simply doesn't work for you and you want to try someone else.

Depending on how much money you spend, you can gain more or less information about your donor. Some banks let you hear the donor's voice or read a letter from them, whereas others only have basic info, such as about the donor's features and health. As I mentioned before, when I called this sort of donation unknown-now-possibly-known-later, if a child is conceived, the child will usually have the right at eighteen to find out more about the donor, including the name and contact details. Some children/families will want this, and others will not, and some may sit on the information a while before deciding. Relationships with donors can change over time, just as most relationships are not static.

Unknown donors are viewed as positive for some families since the donor in that case has no legal rights to your child and is not involved in your life. While some people enjoy having visits with donors or having the donor give their opinion about childrearing, others feel that the fewer people involved, the better. An unknown donor can't be visited and doesn't intrude upon your life. In some countries, it's hard or impossible for LGBTQ+ parents to be on their child's birth certificate if there is a known donor, so using an unknown donor may protect the non-biological parent.

Since donors can donate to multiple people, you may find out that your child has "diblings"—these are donor siblings, or people who share sperm or eggs from the same source. There are even social media groups or other websites that are dedicated to people finding diblings. This may be appealing to you or your child and you may want to go to gatherings for diblings. Or you might feel put off by the idea that other people share genetic material with your child. Or you might be somewhere else on the spectrum, perhaps wanting contacting with one or two diblings but not more, or just once in a while, and so on, and this too can change.

As one of the stories earlier in this book highlighted, some people like the connection to their donor and appreciate access to background information and to the donor and their family. If that's your situation, a known donor might be better. But if you do not want input from more people or if you are concerned about protecting your rights, then an unknown donor might better suit you.

Pros and Cons of an Unknown Donor

PROS	CONS
Egg or sperm donated this way is thoroughly tested.	You usually only get limited information about the donor.
You generally can get access to more information or to the donor when the child turns 18.	Sperm and eggs can be expensive to purchase.
You do not have to another person involved in your and your child's life.	The donor and/or the child may not want contact after the child has turned 18.
There may be biological siblings out there.	There may be biological siblings out there.

A Stor About Choosing an Unknown Donor

As featured before, Perse and Deb are a lesbian couple. Perse already had two children when she and Deb got together. Perse writes about how they chose their donor:

"When we started thinking about how to choose a donor, we initially considered trying to have children that would be biologically related to us both, or to me and the older children. To have children biologically related to both of us, we thought about approaching our brothers—Deb's brother to donate to me, and/or my brother to donate to Deb. When we considered trying to have children related to my kids from my previous (heterosexual) marriage, the idea would have been to ask my ex (my kids' dad) to donate.

However, for a variety of reasons, none of those options felt like the right thing for our future family, so we finally settled on the use of an anonymous donor. We then discovered that the UK had banned anonymous donations some years earlier, and so we eventually came across a sperm bank clinic in Denmark, which was able to deliver its "white gold" to clients throughout the world.

Once we had settled on a source for our donated DNA, we began the search for our preferred donor. The site was set up so that you could search the available donors using a variety of filters including age, occupation, height, education level, eye color, hair color, nationality/ethnicity etc. The parameters we chose reflected a combination of our own and our wider families' traits so, for example, we chose a donor who was tall because all the men in Deb's family are tall, with green eyes (like mine and my kids'), dark, curly hair like both of us, and with a university education, because we have both spent many years in tertiary education, and are both committed life-long learners."

A Story About Choosing an Unknown Donor

Blanche and Esme are a lesbian couple mentioned previously in this book in regard to the laws in France. They left France and decided to move to the UK, where they had their children. They explain their choice of an unknown donor:

"Regarding the decision between known or unknown donor,

being French citizens living in the UK, we were always conscious of what our decisions meant for each legal system. We knew that, for France, a known donor such as a friend, until the adoption approval, would have had parental rights. Even after adoption, some rights over the child would remain. Of course, had we decided to do that, the donor would have been a friend who was happy to delegate all parental responsibilities to us. People, however, change their mind. Had that been the case, our friend would have had solid grounds to obtain at least a right to visit and even shared custody. Right or wrong, we felt it was not entirely impossible that some old homophobic judge might even deem our home unsafe for a child and grant full custody to the donor.

All these considerations played an important part in our decision-making. Despite living in the UK for some time when our first child was born, it was not clear which laws would apply if there was a problem. Choosing an anonymous donor definitely got rid of a lot of uncertainties.

Additionally, we felt, at the time, that having a known donor might also be hard on everyone involved. Hard on the donor, as it must be difficult once the baby is born to not want to be involved and to find their place in the dynamic; hard on the non-biological mother, who might feel their place as a parent challenged; and possibly hard on the child, who would know their donor without necessarily being bound to them by an actual relationship. As a teenager, despite all our efforts in explaining and educating, our child could have found the situation unsettling and might have resented this lack of involvement from the donor. Even though those definitely are not problems that everyone in this situation encounters, we felt that they might be problems for us and the donors we were considering."

Doing it at Home

Whether you use a known donor or an unknown donor, you have to think about how you're going to get the sperm to meet the egg. The main two options are to get the two to hook up either at home or in a fertility clinic.

By "at home," I mean literally in your house, but certainly insemination can also take place in a hotel, in a car, in a bathroom, or any other place where it's legal and safe. No judgement here!

If you're using a known donor, then you'll want to get the sperm-owner to come over, if they don't already live with you, and to produce some sperm. How they do this is up to you and them. It might require nothing more than a hand and an imagination, or they might need a book, magazine, or film, or perhaps a sex toy or a human helper. They'll put the sperm in a sterilized container for you.

If you are using sperm from an unknown donor, you will receive a shipping container with the sperm, probably surrounded by dry ice or liquid nitrogen. You cannot touch the vial with your bare hands, so put on appropriate protective gear. When you're ready to use it, you'll need to thaw the vial. Remember that you can't refreeze a thawed vial of sperm, so be sure you get your timing right.

At this stage, the egg-owner will want to use a syringe (or the old-fashioned turkey baster) to draw up the sperm and insert it into the vaginal canal. Some people like to put in a cervical cap after that, to help retain the sperm inside, but that's up to you. Once the sperm has been injected, you may want to lie still for a while (people often like to rest for 30 to 60 minutes), with your hips raised, to encourage those sperm on their journey. Many people suggest that the egg-owner have an orgasm, as the contractions can help the sperm meet the egg, so if you're in the mood, go for it. An orgasm certainly won't hurt, although you might find the situation slightly unsexy.

Incidentally, some people enjoy putting the sperm in an ejaculating dildo, so they can feel as though their partner is impregnating them and therefore is involved in a physical way. The only issue is ensuring the sperm aren't outside the body too long. If you've paid a lot of money for the sperm, you might worry about wasting sperm by moving it from one container to another and potentially not getting it all into the vaginal canal in the end.

Regardless of whether you use known or unknown donor sperm and whether you're inseminating at home or in a clinic, you will need to track your ovulation patterns. It is generally a waste of time and money to inseminate when you're not ovulating, as you'd have a low chance of pregnancy. See Appendix 1 for an ovulation chart (or you can use an app), which will help you track your temperature, cervical mucus, cycle, and so on.

You cannot fertilize an egg in one body and then move it to a different uterus at home. So, if you plan to use sperm from one person, an egg from another, and the uterus of a third, you'll have to go to a clinic.

Pros and Cons of Doing It at Home

PROS	CONS
It can be comfortable being in your own space, or a space of your choosing.	It can also be weird or off-putting to inseminate in your own home or to know you have a sperm-owner masturbating in the next room.
You have a lot of flexibility about where and how to produce the sperm and to inseminate.	You are limited in that the egg-owner and the uterus-owner have to be the same person.
You don't have to spend lots of money on a clinic.	You have to make sure you get the timing right.
Your partner can inseminate you.	You can't test the sperm for STIs at home.

A Stor, About Making Your Bab, at Home

MKK, who is butch and queer, and her wife, who is bisexual and genderfluid, inseminated at home. She describes their situation:

"We had a known donor, a close friend of mine from college. He froze his sperm at a sperm bank in his city and then it was shipped to the branch of the sperm bank in our city so that I could pick up the tanks each month and bring them home on public transit.

We tried for three months unassisted using ICI vials (intra-cervical insemination) and then switched to at-home unmedicated IUI (intrauterine insemination) with the help of a midwife. She got everything set up and then let me push the little plunger on the syringe, so I could honestly tell our kid that I helped to make him.

The apartment where we conceived him wound up being across the street from his preschool, so even though he never got to see inside (we moved to a different apartment before he was born), it was fun to be able to point out the building where we made him on our way to and from school.

Our donor and his spouse come to our city to visit whenever they can, and we go to their city as often as our schedule allows. My wife and I have complicated relationships with our parents, so for a while our son's closest grandparent was our donor's spouse's mom, who asked him to call her "Gaga." It was wonderful to have that warmth and acceptance from someone who was several steps removed from our son genetically, but nevertheless considered him part of the family."

Fertility Clinics

If you don't want to do it at home or if you have underlying fertility issues (besides not having all the necessary biological material or equipment), you may choose to use a fertility clinic.

At a clinic, you will have a variety of choices. For one thing, you may consider whether to have an IUI, IVF, ICSI, or reciprocal IVF. An IUI is intrauterine insemination, and it is when the sperm is placed into the uterus, where it will hopefully be accepted by an egg. Sometimes you have the option to do this in an unmedicated way (also called a natural cycle), where your ovulation is tracked, and the sperm is placed inside at the right time. In some cases, you will need medication to stimulate the ovaries to produce an egg or two and to ovulate.

IVF is in-vitro fertilization. Your body is stimulated to make eggs, then the eggs are removed and placed in a petri dish or similar together with the sperm. The hope is that the eggs will welcome the sperm and for multiple embryos to be formed in this way. Any eggs and sperm that fuse into embryos are watched for a couple of days and then either implanted in the uterus or frozen for use another time.

ICSI goes one step further. It stands for intracytoplasmic sperm injection, and it is where a clinician inserts a single sperm into a single egg. Often, this is done if there are known issues with the sperm, such as low sperm count or abnormally shaped sperm, among other possibilities.

Reciprocal IVF (also called partner-shared fertility treatment or partner-assisted treatment) is where a two-uterus family can share the experience. One of the partners can have their eggs collected, fertilized, and then transferred to the other. This may make both partners feel involved and/or might also be a necessity, if, for example, one partner has a low egg reserve, or one would find it too dysphoric to get pregnant.

Options at a Fertility Clinic

TERM	DEFINITION
IUI (intrauterine insemination)	Sperm is placed into the uterus.
IVF (in-vitro fertilization)	Eggs removed from the body are placed with the sperm outside of the body. The resulting blastocyst[4] is placed in the body.
ICSI (intracytoplasmic sperm injection)	A single sperm is inserted into a single egg.
R-IVF (reciprocal IVF)	Eggs from one partner are removed and fertilized, then placed in another partner.
FET (a frozen embryo transfer)	The blastocyst is frozen and placed in the gestational parent at a later point.

Besides thinking about the approach, you may also get a choice about whether to do this medicated or not and, if you do use medication, how much you want to use. In an unmedicated approach to an IUI, as already mentioned, you follow what your body does naturally. This is not possible for IVF, where the aim is usually to get more than just one or two eggs. Some people may not want to or be able to do it unmedicated for an IUI either. You might also make the request to use a lower dose of medications; for example, if you know you don't want loads of frozen embryos for the future or if you are breastfeeding/chestfeeding while undergoing fertility treatment and feel more comfortable with fewer drugs in your system, especially as they might decrease your milk supply.

You may also choose whether to transfer a fresh embryo or a frozen one (a frozen embryo transfer is called a FET). A fresh transfer is where the blastocyst is transferred to you soon after egg

---

4 A blastocyst is the term for the early structure, while the word embryo is technically employed when there's an amniotic sac, which happens around 10 to 12 days after fertilization. A blastocyst is usually transferred five to seven days after fertilization.

collection, usually three or five days later. In a frozen transfer, the embryos are frozen (in a high-grade medical freezer) and can be transferred days, weeks, months, or years later. It could be that there are reasons why your clinic recommends you do one or the other sort of transfer or it could be purely pragmatic for you, such as if you are going on vacation or have a work trip scheduled directly after egg collection and won't be able to have a fresh transfer. Also, after you have a baby, you can wait some months or years and then have a FET to hopefully produce the next child.

Another choice is whether to test your embryos before transferring them. This might be done if someone has previously had multiple miscarriages or if there have been some issues with the egg, sperm, or embryos. Testing them can provide information about the DNA, including the sex. This may or may not be something you wish to know.

Now, it must be said; you may not actually have all these choices that I just outlined. Some might be made for you, because of your circumstances or because of what your clinic offers. Ideally, you would feel that all this was happening in consultation with your clinic, rather than something that is done to you by the clinic and the fertility experts.

As you can probably tell, there are often many options available at a clinic. Partly because of that and partly because fertility clinics are not always considered medically necessary (some view them as a luxury since humans don't have a "right" to have children), well, there's no other way to say this; using fertility clinics can get very costly. Every time you walk through their doors, you will be charged. There are costs for appointments, for tests, medications, treatments, counseling, and so on. Some places will even charge you if they send you an email or if they phone you up to give you a brief piece of information, such as whether your blastocysts formed. Given how specialized the field is and how it is for-profit, fees can range widely and can be jaw-droppingly high.

There are ways of defraying or decreasing costs, however. Some clinics will allow you to use your own doctor's office to undergo basic blood tests, and this might be free or cheaper than the clinic's costs, whereas other clinics will insist that you have to do it in their offices. You can also buy packages for treatment, such as a certain number of attempts at IVF for a lower sum than if you had to pay for each treatment separately, but of course, it is a gamble. If you pay for a slightly discounted rate for three IVF attempts but end up being successful during your first attempt, then you will have paid much more and you will lose out. On the other hand, if a baby isn't conceived from any of your attempts, you might get some money back, but that doesn't really make up for the fact that you don't have your longed-for baby. Also, most clinics have rules around who can buy these packages; you usually need be approved based on your health and age. One other way of getting treatment at a lower rate is by donating biological material, usually eggs. Many clinics don't have enough donor eggs, and if you are young and healthy enough, they will happily take some of yours and then give you free or discounted treatment.

I already mentioned how, at fertility clinics, you will be required to undergo—usually at your own expense—many tests, including for sexually transmitted infections (STIs), among other things. You might find some of this intrusive and embarrassing. In some cases, it can feel downright bizarre. If one of the partners in a relationship isn't contributing biological material to make a baby, what does it matter what their blood type or STI status is? Is it because clinics in particular or people in general are worried about children growing up with parents who have sexually transmitted diseases? People who procreate at home in the traditional way aren't subjected to these kinds of checks. Besides this, you may be expected to undergo counselling and/or to discuss some personal matters with nurses, doctors, and other staff. People have mentioned being asked about their family backgrounds, sex lives, religious beliefs, and more, and some felt they were judged, depending on their responses.

Finally, you should carefully explore what your clinic and country's rules are regarding how long they will store eggs, sperm, and embryos and how much they charge for it. They may also have rules about whether you can move your biological material from one clinic to another, or even to another country, and whether any sperm or egg donors will have a say over what happens. So, ensure you know what the stance is beforehand so you're ready for the future.

In sum, there's a lot to think about with clinics. Though some people are entitled to free treatment at clinics, mostly they are businesses that aim to make a profit. As such, they charge a lot. Ideally, these fees would mean that they treat everyone who comes through their doors professionally and respectfully, but as we LGBTQ+ folks know, this isn't always a given. I will never forget that the clinic stamped this notice on our records: "Diagnosis: Same-Sex Couple." I found that offensive and thoughtless, as if they were saying we were diseased merely because we were queer. Be prepared, in other words, both for a big bill and potentially to have to insist on being treated with basic human decency.

Pros and Cons of Fertility Clinics

PROS	CONS
You will receive medical attention, which may be necessary depending on your situation.	Your clinician/consultant may not approve of or accept your wishes.
Everything is done in a clinical setting, with medical tests and attention to detail.	You may find a clinic to be a sterile, uninviting environment.
You will have some choices about how your baby is conceived.	Your path will most likely involve medication. They may have side effects.

Professionals who you are paying ought to treat you fairly and respectfully.	Not all clinics or doctors are LGBTQ+-friendly.
Medical treatment may help you conceive more quickly or easily.	You may find some of the questions, tests, or treatments intrusive or uncomfortable.
Depending on where you live or on your situation, you may be eligible for lower fees or free treatment.	Fertility treatment is often costly, although there are sometimes ways to defray the costs.

A Stor, from Someone Who Had a Difficult Experience With a Fertilit, Clinic

Nichola, a gay woman, first tried to get pregnant with a known donor and unfortunately miscarried. Then, her partner tried to get pregnant at a fertility clinic, but they found this unpleasant. Finally, Nichola inseminated at home with her partner's brother's sperm. She explains their journey this way:

"At the age of 38, I miscarried. I had asked a friend to be a donor and we self-inseminated at home. The pregnancy had lasted 9 weeks. I was devastated to miscarry, but I knew that the method could work. The following year, after I'd put a lot of pressure on my partner, we went to a fertility clinic in our city. I had persuaded her to be the one to go through the treatment.

The fertility consultant was religious man. It was evident from his questions and comments that he was a homophobe, maybe because of his religious beliefs. For instance, he asked us (a female couple) how often we had sex. Presumably, this is a standard and relevant question when treating a heterosexual couple who are having trouble conceiving, but we were surprised by this question, as no matter how many times we had sex, it would not result in a pregnancy. He then went on to tell us that he knew, and named, the kinds of things "you people" do in the bedroom. During one consultation, he told us, "We *have* to treat you people now because of the pink pound."

When explaining the technicality of the treatment, he finished by saying, "And with God's help, it will work." My partner and I said that it was surely science and not God that would determine its efficacy, but the consultant appeared appalled and said, "How *have* you people been brought up?"

The treatment did not work, we were left £6000 poorer, and we felt humiliated by the whole process. Sometime after this, my partner logged our experience with Stonewall.

Three years later, after a chance encounter with an old friend who had had a baby when she thought she was actually going through menopause, we decided to give it one last shot. I was 43 so knew my chances of conceiving and carrying a healthy baby were slim. This time, we asked my partner's brother if he would consider being a donor for us. We thought it would be great if a child could be genetically linked to the both of us. He kindly agreed after only five minutes of deliberation.

He and I both had sexual health screening at the local hospital. After being scorched by the private clinic, we decided to self-inseminate at home again. The second month that we tried it, it worked!

We now have a healthy, happy 5-year-old daughter. She says that she loves having two mums and a dad. We have parental and financial responsibility for our daughter, and she gets to do fun things with her dad once a week. Occasionally, I get annoyed with her dad for feeding her crap or buying clothes that I think are inappropriate, and she's always a little bit naughtier after a day with him because he doesn't encourage manners and doesn't discipline her, but otherwise, it's worked out really well."

A Stor, Involving Three Fertilit, Clinics

Perse and Deb are a lesbian couple who have already shared a bit in this book about their journey. They first used two fertility clinics in the UK and then a third in New Zealand. Perse discusses their experiences:

"Our experience with our first fertility clinic came after three failed attempts at at-home insemination and was awful. The clinicians (both doctors and nurses) made no attempt to create a happy, welcoming atmosphere for us, failed to explain the purpose of the (expensive and invasive) proce- dures, and got our names wrong on numerous occasions. The final straw came when Deb was told that in order to proceed with her IVF, I would be required to undertake a battery of tests to assess my fertility!

The fact that the clinic had completely failed to acknowl- edge our lesbian relationship, and thoughtlessly applied policies and procedures designed for male partners of women undergoing fertility treatment was, to me, a horri- ble, psychologically annihilating experience. We felt unseen, uncared for, and while Deb was so unimportant to them that they got her name wrong on two separate occasions, I was reduced to being her "pseudo-husband" whose personal fertility (sperm count?) was apparently "relevant" to my wife's ongoing treatment plan.

As a result of our fraught, demeaning, and expensive expe- rience, we decided to find an alternative clinic to continue our IVF journey, eventually setting on a London-based clinic.

Our experience was a lot more positive, and the nursing staff were kind and attentive at each and every appoint- ment we attended (the doctors were kind but brusque). We undertook a full IVF round, with a fresh embryo trans- fer (unsuccessful), followed by two more attempts using frozen embryos. The first frozen embryo transfer (FET) was unsuccessful, but the second one (a double embryo transfer) resulted in a pregnancy, which, sadly, ended in miscarriage at 8 weeks' gestation.

By the time we experienced our miscarriage, we had moved to Aotearoa New Zealand, and engaged our third fertility clinic to help us on our journey to pregnancy. The clinic itself was tiny by comparison to the ones we had used in the UK, and the doctors, nurses, and support staff (receptionists, administrators, etc.) were all incredibly friendly, kind, and supportive. The whole set-up was completely different to the UK, feeling so much more homely and inviting, and with all staff being openly supportive and non-judgmental of our relationship. Even the tone of the appointment follow-up letters was different, and everything conspired to make us feel welcome, confident, and part of the fertility clinic family.

The difference for Deb was clear when she had her first FET, which in the UK had been a fraught and painful experience, but in the welcoming and comfortable context of our third clinic, was calm, painless, and a beautiful, celebratory experience that the doctor fully shared with us.

Our three clinic experiences spanned the full range of experiences from appalling, through adequate, to wonderful. Being truly seen, accepted, and cared for as women on an exciting, demanding, and emotional journey to motherhood, as opposed to being seen and treated as cash cows (clinic one) or items on a factory conveyor belt (clinic two), was transformational and the proof in the pudding was two successful pregnancies in wonderful Aotearoa New Zealand."

A Story About Reciprocal IVF

Jess and Laila, a lesbian couple, conceived using reciprocal IVF. Jess describes their choice this way:

"Our journey started 6 years ago, when we met. We knew we were going to be lifelong partners and knew that having children would require some planning and preparing. From the start, we knew that we wanted to have an anonymous donor and so we began our search privately through a clinic.

We were also keen to try reciprocal IVF and luckily enough, met the criteria to have this option, whilst donating eggs to another female recipient.

It was easy for us to decide who would carry the baby, as one of us had no desire to carry a baby, and the other couldn't wait! We are aware that this isn't always the case for some couples.

Our clinic was extremely helpful and supportive of LGBT couples. We were fortunate to get pregnant in the first round of doing IVF. We felt it was important for us both to be part of our child's journey, which meant one of us donating the eggs, with the other carrying the baby. This was the best decision that we made."

A Story from a Couple Who Donated Eggs

Ellen, a lesbian, and Rhiannon, a bisexual woman, have three children. Rhiannon carried the first child and then Ellen carried two, who were twins, with all three children having the same source for both sperm and eggs. Rhiannon donated her eggs to fund their treatment. Ellen describes their journey as follows:

"When we first decided we wanted to become parents we attended an LGBTQ Parenting Show. It was so helpful in showing us options: adopt, foster, own children with known donor, own children with anonymous donor, using a registered clinic, DIY turkey baster, etc. We knew we wanted to raise children with no ongoing contact or involvement from a father/donor. We listened to a presentation from a family lawyer who explained that if we used a known donor plus DIY turkey baster, there was a chance the donor could contest us both being parents and the non-birth mother would not be on the birth certificate. We were fortunate that we could afford the alternative option of fertility treatment at a registered clinic, and we decided to go for it. What appealed to us was we would be the sole parents; we would both be on the birth certificate and the donor was screened for health issues.

There were clinic representatives at the Parenting Show, and we found one in our area. Our initial plan was that my partner would carry our first child with her eggs and in a few years, I would carry our second child with my eggs and the same donor, making the children half-siblings. We decided my partner would try treatment first because she was older and therefore, her clock was ticking faster (turns out, her clock was just fine). We were presented with so many options—IUI, IVF, blastocyst, freezing embryos, egg sharing—and honestly it was quite overwhelming. For us, we felt due to the financial and emotional investment, we wanted the option that had the greatest chance of success (and the most expensive): IVF with blastocyst.

As my partner's eggs were plentiful and great quality, we decided to egg share (she gave half the eggs collected to another woman). This brought the cost of treatment down significantly, making it more affordable for us. We were so lucky that we were successful the first time and after one round of IVF, we had a baby (and the egg recipient's treatment was successful too).

Fast-forward 18 months and we wanted to add to our family—my turn. We had planned to do just the same as with my partner. We discovered after one unsuccessful round of IVF that I had limited eggs, and they were poor quality so not only was egg sharing not an option, but the consultant recommended if we wanted to try again, we should consider using my partner's eggs. It was quite a big blow for me, and we had to decide whether to just keep on trying with me and my eggs whilst weighing up what we could afford and at what point we would call it quits.

I was keen to experience pregnancy and carrying a child, so we decided to try IVF with my partner's eggs, transferred to me. Again, she did egg sharing, and we were thrilled to find out I was carrying twins (and the donor recipient's treatment was successful too).

We now have a 6-year-old and 4-year-old twins, and we are so happy with our family. We are exceptionally lucky to have been successful and to afford the treatment. We were treated well by the clinic. The tough parts for us were not really knowing what was going on during the treatment. There are so many tests and expenses, and nothing happens quickly, even in a private clinic. Having to inject hormones and prepare your body for egg stimulation and retrieval is tiring and at each stage we became more and more invested, which made the low of unsuccessful treatment really hard.

Another consideration for us is that just as our children can seek out the sperm donor if they choose when they are 18, so can the children born from my partner's eggs. We are prepared for that, but it will certainly be a new dynamic if they would like to build a relationship with her (of course, they may not. They may not even ever find out they are donor eggs). As for our children, they understand I was the "tummy mummy" for the twins and that they are full siblings, which I think is lovely.

I am a little sad that treatment with my eggs didn't work so there are no little "mes" but as my children grow, I see my influences and the result of "nurture" so am less concerned they don't have my genes. They don't care whose genes they have; they just love that we are there to give them cuddles with a story on our laps."

Surrogacy or Gestational Carrying

Surrogacy is where you borrow or rent someone's womb. The surrogate—sometimes also called a gestational carrier—is not typically biologically related to the baby (in other words, they have not usually also provided the egg) and they will not be a parent to the child. Surrogates are typically employed in situations where there is no uterus in the family, as in a two-dad set-up, or where there is a uterus, but the owner of that uterus is not able or willing to use it to gestate the baby. There are some cases where the carrier of the baby has also donated the egg to make the baby, but in general, full surrogacy means there is no biological connection.

As surrogacy is relatively new, there are varying rules, laws, and norms around many aspects of it, such as payment, who can be a surrogate, or contact with the surrogate. But even though it is new, it's already a quickly growing field, with numbers quadrupling in the last decade in the UK (Deahl, 2021).

You need to consider whether you want your surrogate to be a friend or acquaintance or someone you don't know at all. In other words, what sort of relationship do you want to have with the surrogate and how do you anticipate it developing? How closely connected to the surrogate do you want to be? Will you do this in your country or abroad? Will the surrogate provide human milk? Will your child get to meet the surrogate and know the surrogate's role in their life? Will you regularly send the surrogate pictures of your child? And so on. Before you talk to potential surrogates, decide what would work best for you and your family, and then have open conversations with the surrogate so you agree about this.

If your surrogate is a friend or relative, you'll already know them and be able to talk through these issues. But if you don't know who your surrogate will be, you will need to try to find one. There are social media groups dedicated to helping surrogates match with those who need them, and there are also agencies and nonprofit organizations that connect people. Laws differ. For instance, "Surrogacy is legal in the UK. However, it is illegal to advertise for a surrogate and it is illegal for third parties to profit from matching" while in the US, "commercial surrogacy is legal in many states" (Deahl, 2021).

Once you have found a possible surrogate, you will need to ascertain whether they fit the recommended guidelines for surrogacy. For example, some fertility clinics only allow certain people to be surrogates. In general, they have to be people over a certain age and under another age. This is due to the desire to optimize the situation by having a surrogate who is generally healthy. For this reason, some clinics have rules around body mass index (BMI) as well, which some people find upsetting and inappropriate, because someone can be healthy, even with a higher BMI. Many clinics say that someone cannot be a surrogate if they don't already have children of their own, presumably because of concerns about a surrogate getting attached to a baby and potentially not wanting to give it to the parents after birth. Many clinics also have recommendations or rules around residency, smoking and drug status, and mental illness, so check with your specific clinic. You may also have your own ideas about what you are looking for in a surrogate. I have seen several people ask for a surrogate or offer themselves as a surrogate and specifically mention their ethnicity, which some other people find ethically dubious. You will have to decide for yourself, in consultation with your clinic and your surrogate, about what you want and need from a surrogate.

Besides practical concerns like that, you will want to think about the emotional and legal aspects. Many clinics require the surrogate to have some counselling, sometimes together with the intended parents, to ensure that this situation will work. Both you and the surrogate will want to have strong support networks around you. From a legal standpoint, you may need to check the laws and/or involve a lawyer to be certain that the surrogate won't automatically go on the birth certificate or, if they do, that they will surrender their rights and give you parental responsibility. Besides that, you will want to talk about some potentially hard things, such as who would make decisions about antenatal testing, abortion, interventions, and so forth. Talk to the surrogate about what would happen if you came into conflict and couldn't agree on a way forward. Some of the topics in Appendix 2 will be useful to you; those are about a known donor, but many can be applied to surrogacy too.

Also, different countries have different opinions about whether to pay surrogates or not and, if so, how much. So, you will need to consider costs, which may include covering fertility treatment, the surrogate's antenatal healthcare, maternity clothing, hospital fees, lost income from time off employment, and more. In *Three Dads and a Baby*, Ian Jenkins writes about how he and his two partners used a donor egg and a surrogate to make their children, and he calculates the cost for the first child to be over $120,000. Many people simply couldn't afford that or would need to go seriously into debt to do that. On the other hand, as he points out, being a poly family perhaps means that there is more income available to spend on child-making and childrearing. In your own case, you will probably want to calculate projected costs ahead of time, to ensure it is a viable option for you. Given that there always unforeseen circumstances and costs, add in extra. For instance, the baby might be born prematurely, and both the baby and the surrogate might need extra care, plus the surrogate may expect compensation for any additional time taken off work.

Along with this, you will want to discuss with the surrogate what your expectations are for the birth and afterwards. Make sure you and the surrogate are open about your feelings, so you are both (or all) fully part of the process. Will you attend the birth? Who will be the first person to hold the baby? Will the surrogate chestfeed/breastfeed or express for the baby? What happens if the baby and/or the surrogate is ill after birth?

As with sperm or egg donation, using a surrogate or loaning out one's uterus is not always an easy decision to make. Having a lot of conversations about the situation in advance will really help you as you progress down this route.

Pros and Cons of Surrogacy

PROS	CONS
A friend or acquaintance loans you their uterus, which helps if you don't have one or can't or won't use yours.	There are often regulations about who can be a surrogate, so it can be hard to find one.
You might have a connection or develop a bond or relationship with your surrogate.	The costs can be prohibitive.
It can be a great way to have a biological child.	You will likely be tied into using a clinic or medical facility.[5]
You get a chance to have in-depth conversations before birth about how you want your parenting situation to look.	There may be some practical, emotional, and ethical concerns to work through.

Surrogacy and Infant Feeding

Zoe Faulkner is an IBCLC who has been Chair of Lactation Consultants of Great Britain (LCGB) since 2015, representing the organization nationally and internationally, with a keen interest in equality and diversity issues. She has spoken at many conferences and is a Breastfeeding Peer Support Coordinator for Sussex Community NHS Foundation Trust in Brighton and Hove, England, where she manages, trains, and supervises around 40 volunteers at any one time. She is a heterosexual, cisgender woman, a carer and mother,

---

5 Unless your surrogate is also using their own eggs and you inseminate at home.

and, as a person with dyslexia, is part of the neurodiverse community. She can be found at www.brightonbreastfeeding.co.uk.

Zoe sums up the issues around surrogates providing human milk when she writes:

"When it comes to human milk feeding, there are a number of considerations for the intended parent, gestational carrier, and lactation consultant to navigate. Remembering that in the U.S., providing human milk may be part of the agreement between the intended parents and gestational carrier, the current difference in the legal system in the UK means that this has not been commonly explored. The intended parents may fear the gestational carrier bonding with the baby and not signing over parental responsibility.

One of the ethical considerations is that the baby should be the priority, so ideally, they would receive the gestational carrier's milk should they lactate. This means that the option of donating human milk via a milk bank rather than providing it for the baby would go against the principles and ethical frameworks involved. There are also the health implications of abrupt weaning for the gestational carrier, remembering that lactation following pregnancy reduces the risk of pre-menopausal breast cancer."

A Story About Surrogacy

Nicki and Anna are a gay couple. Their family-creation journey has included fertility treatment, IUIs, miscarriage, reciprocal IVF, and surrogacy. Here, Nicki writes about their path to surrogacy:

"I had always wanted to be a mother of multiple children and I'm pretty sure that by the end of our first date, Anna was aware of this. We decided to get ourselves on the waiting list for government-funded IVF (through the National Health Service in the UK) the year before we got married in the hope that we could then start our family soon after our wedding. As it happened, the NHS fertility services in our area had a complete reshuffle, there were massive waiting lists, and they changed the criteria for lesbian couples being eligible for treatment before we reached the top, so we ended up going privately.

When discussing which of us would be pregnant, the conversation went something like this:

Nicki: I've always wanted to be pregnant.

Anna: I've never wanted to be pregnant.

Both: Well, that was an easy decision then.

We decided to try IUI and on our 4th attempt, I became pregnant. We were so delighted and three weeks after we saw the double line on the test, we eagerly went for our early pregnancy scan, only to find out that the pregnancy was not viable, as there was no fetal pole (the start of a baby) growing inside the sac. This pregnancy resulted in miscarriage, and we were both devastated.

As a couple where the only issue was a lack of sperm, we had assumed it would all be pretty straightforward. But the constant waiting—for your period, for a scan, for follicles to grow, for the lining to thicken, to see how your body responds to this drug or that, for insemination day, for test day, and so on—really got to me. Then there was that utterly awful wait after the scan when we were told it was almost certainly not viable but that they had to scan again in seven days to confirm.

This whole process made me feel hugely out of control and I didn't feel like I could keep going with it month after month. Anna had also realized, during those three weeks when we believed we were pregnant and were going to have this baby, that a small part of her was sad that she would have no genetic link to the child. So, after a short break to recover physically and to mentally pick ourselves back up, we decided to switch to reciprocal IVF, which would give us much higher chances of success than IUI.

In 2014, our first child was born, created from Anna's egg and donor sperm and carried by me. James was conceived from our first attempt at IVF, the pregnancy was smooth, albeit with a lot of morning (and afternoon and evening) sickness, and the birth was a wonderful, drug-free, hospital birth, pretty much how we'd planned it to be. Three-and-a-half weeks later, however, I suffered a large hemorrhage, caused by some undetected retained placenta and I had to have an emergency D&C (dilation and curettage) to save my life. This was the start of our fertility issues.

The D&C caused trauma to my uterus, resulting in dense scarring (Asherman's Syndrome) to 80% of it, and I was, therefore, not likely to be able to carry another pregnancy. At this point, you might think that the obvious solution would be for Anna to carry our next child. However, Anna has never felt a desire to be pregnant, as it's just not her, and I still felt that I wanted to be.

So, I went through two surgeries to clear my uterus and a lot of hormone treatment in order for me to be able to grow our family. In 2018, our second child, Andrew, was born. This pregnancy was definitely not smooth; there were complications, bleeding, high risks, the baby was breech due to my uterus not being optimal for him to turn around, and we were relieved when he was born safely via emergency C-section at 36+5 weeks. This time, the surgeon could clearly see that the placenta was not coming away as it should and tried, unsuccessfully, to clear it but again, I hemorrhaged. Three months later, I had further surgery with my specialist, and it was at this point that he informed me that it was not worth the risks for me to attempt a third pregnancy.

This news was crushing. We had seven frozen embryos and we were not ready to give up on our desire for a third child but equally, Anna did not feel that she could be the one to go through pregnancy. My specialist said that surrogacy was another option. It was hard for me to accept that Anna was unwilling to be pregnant whilst I would have done almost anything to be able to. I also felt that it was unfair to ask someone to be our surrogate when Anna had the physical ability to carry our baby and we already had two children.

However, a good friend of mine, Jamielee, had wanted to be a surrogate for many years and had mentioned this to me previously. When I spoke to her and tentatively asked whether she might consider being a surrogate for us, she quickly replied that she'd "be honored to." Many conversations followed and there was much research into how we would go about a surrogacy arrangement. While we were all excited to move forward with this, there was also much anxiety.

Legally in the UK, there is no requirement for a couple to be infertile in order to have a child through surrogacy. However, in the surrogacy community, it was clear that we weren't welcome as a couple choosing surrogacy rather than being a couple who had no other option. I was spoken to rudely in Facebook groups and we were ineligible to join Surrogacy UK, one of the few legal surrogacy agencies in this country, which many couples and individuals use in order to hopefully meet someone who will be their surrogate.

I learned not to share the details of why we were considering surrogacy and accepted that I would not find another same-sex female couple to chat with. Our fertility clinic had also never been in this situation, and they questioned whether they could treat us. The view is that it is unethical to put someone through the risks of treatment and pregnancy in order to have a baby for another person when that person is able to do it themselves. Our situation, therefore, had to be put through the clinic's ethics committee before we were given permission to go ahead. In the end, they decided that it would be discrimination to deny me treatment, as an infertile woman, due to my sexuality, i.e., if I was in a heterosexual relationship and infertile, I would have been able to access treatment using a surrogate and, therefore, should not be denied it due to being married to a woman.

Once approved, our treatment went smoothly, and we were thrilled that the first embryo transfer resulted in pregnancy. Our third child was born in 2020. She is a pandemic baby, conceived only weeks before the country locked down. Many families struggled with pregnancy during lockdown with partners unable to attend appointments or scans. In our case, it seemed particularly cruel that neither parent could attend, and I know Jamielee felt terrible having to attend alone. We were, however, given permission for both me and Anna to be at the birth along with a birth partner for Jamielee. As it was, Jamielee didn't want a birth partner and Anna was unable to get there in time for the birth, and so, it was just myself and Jamielee present, with Anna on the phone, at that most magical moment when Elin entered the world.

Being LGBTQ+ was never an issue. I felt like most people we encountered, be they professionals, friends, or strangers, were interested and curious but I can't think of any negative experiences. Perhaps it was because we never had all three of us women (Jamielee, Anna, and myself) at any appoint-ment after the early pregnancy scan.

It was certainly different experiencing our pregnancy from the other side. I did not miss the morning sickness or heartburn, but it was hard to know that someone else was feeling the first kicks and I felt immensely guilty when Jamielee was feeling sick, tired, or in pain. I must say that Jamielee was utterly amazing throughout the whole process, never complained, and did everything she could to make it clear to everyone that this was not her baby and that we were the parents."

A Story from the Surrogate's Side

Jamielee is a heterosexual woman who served as the surrogate for Nicki and Anna. She writes about her experience:

"For as long as I can remember, I have always wanted to be a surrogate. My husband and I had several conversations about it before we got married and I was over the moon to discover that he was behind me 1000%.

I didn't know my surrogate journey would start by me having a child for an LGBTQ+ family; I always thought it would be for a family member. After I had met Nicki, we started talking about how she wanted another child and seeing how hard the journey was for her with everything she had to go through to conceive, I knew then that Anna and Nicki were the perfect couple to have a child for.

Then one day, I told Nicki that I would love to be a surrogate and we used to joke about if she couldn't conceive her second child, then I would carry for her. Unfortunately, after Nicki had her second child, she was told she couldn't carry any more children, so I then offered to be their surrogate.

This surrogate journey was one of the most amazing and rewarding things I could have ever done. The best thing was living so close to each other so that Anna and Nicki's children could also be involved in the pregnancy."

Co-Parenting

Co-parenting or shared parenting basically means two or more adults who take on financial, legal, and/or moral responsibility for raising and socializing one or more children. But in practice, it can play out in a variety of ways.

Couples can produce a child together and then separate, so they share parental responsibility, even if they are no longer in a relationship. They might continue to live together, or they might live separately, so the child moves between homes, or else the child might stay in one home for the sake of simplicity and consistency, and the parents are the ones who take turns. Co-parenting in this situation can vary, from parents who don't want to be in a relationship but are happy to spend holidays together and to take trips as a family to parents who can barely stand the sight of one another and only communicate to discuss practical matters relating to the children, if even that.

Another kind of coparenting is potentially a bit queerer, in that it doesn't have to involve romance or sex, which challenges our usual societal ideas about what romantic or sexual relationships are for and about what a family looks like. This is where a couple or a group of people decide to produce a child together and to share financial and practical responsibility for the child. An example would be a gay male couple who donate sperm to a gay female couple, where the plan is for the child to divide time between the two homes, or perhaps for everyone to live together, or maybe for the child to primarily live with one set of adults but also to know and spend time with the other. Another example would be people in a platonic relationship who both, or all, want a child. Yet another situation would be a cooperative, where one or more children live with and are raised by a number of adults, and not everyone is biologically or legally connected to everyone else.

Whatever co-parenting might look like in your specific situation, it'd be beneficial for all the adults to have similar views on how family life will be or what sorts of rules or guidelines you want for the child/children. It's confusing for children to have, for instance, one parent who is permissive and another who is strict, or to have to try to remember what they're allowed to eat, wear, or do in one household versus another. It's also important that parents not put down the other adults involved in the co-parenting constellation or to force a child into the middle of an antagonistic relationship. Lots of open discussions are needed, something that's arguably true of all families, and those discussions should include the child too, as they get older. It may also be worthwhile having a non-legally binding agreement before pregnancy or adoption, as with known donors (see Appendix 2). As in every situation, there will probably be some challenges, so being flexible and open and willing to talk is key.

You will probably also want to have a schedule, so you know who is doing what with the child and when. While this might be tricky for more spontaneous types of people, it can simplify life. It also means that you are more likely to get a break from parenting and to be able to focus on your work, hobbies, or relationships when your child is with another adult.

Pros and Cons of Co-Parenting

PROS	CONS
More adults to love and take responsibility for the children.	More adults who need to agree on rules and strategies.
Co-parenting focuses on the child rather than on intimate/romantic relationships.	Some people prefer to raise children in the context of intimate/romantic relationships.
Co-parenting can challenge societal ideas.	Some outsiders might make awkward or rude comments about co-parenting set-ups.

Depending on your set-up, you might get some time off from parenting.	You will probably need clear schedules and boundaries.
Parenting may be less stressful, since others will be able to contribute time and money.	If you wanted to move to another location, that might not be possible, depending on your agreement with your coparent/s.

A Stor, about Co-Parenting

H is a queer/bisexual polyamorous woman who produced and raises her son, F, in a co-parenting relationship. H describes how this situation developed and how she feels about it:

"At the moment, I have two long-term partners, neither of whom are the father of my child. The story of how my son came to be conceived makes more sense told from the beginning, so here we go.

From the age of 13, I defined as a lesbian. I exclusively had relationships with women (except for some brief exploration) and I enthusiastically threw myself into local queer culture. I went to LGBTQ+ clubs, youth groups, and events. I consumed lots of queer media and I cultivated a wide circle of queer friends. I was blessed to have a family who accepted me and as such felt I could be a spokesperson for lesbian youth, appearing on some national TV documentaries and radio shows, in a popular youth magazine, and speaking at conferences about my experiences. I was as lesbian as they come.

These experiences, combined with knowing from a young age that I wanted children, meant that I had thought a great deal about alternative family structures. It's not as simple as just wanting children when you're LGBTQ+; they're unlikely to happen by accident and the options for having them by design are broad. I already knew all about donor insemination, whether by a local donor or through a clinic, and had spoken extensively with a gay male friend as a potential donor/coparent by the age of 18.

My keenness to get started on a family was never shared by my partners though, who always had a laundry list of life events they wanted to get through first. I didn't share their view that life stopped when you had kids, but as we were monogamous, it had to be a team decision, so I waited.

Imagine my surprise, then, when I fell for a man when I was 27. S was poly, autistic, and unlike anyone I'd ever met. As he talked to me about polyamory, I recognized a pattern in myself that I had never given attention to before and a great many things fell into place. I rather abruptly broke off my monogamous, cohabiting, lesbian relationship of three years and adopted a bisexual, polyamorous life with gusto.

S and I both wanted kids immediately. We also had all the relevant body parts! But in a fit of common sense, we decided not to go ahead straight away. We set a review date six months ahead to check in with what we wanted to do, and by then, we had split up. We congratulated ourselves on not acting on our impulses and continued being friends. We also both continued being poly, and then when a room came up in my queer shared house, S moved in. From there, we started brewing the idea of setting up a housing co-op to give our queer family-of-friends good quality, affordable housing.

As our lives got more intertwined and it became clear that our ideas about parenting overlapped a lot, the idea started surfacing again. None of our partners wanted to have children but they didn't want to hold us back either. We were already planning to live together in the long term. The nature of polyamory meant that we had a great network of support around us. I considered going the donor route but as I am not close to my bio family, I felt it was better to give my child another parent and the extended family that he brought with him. Within 6 months, we had a baby on the way.

We started having meetings to set up our housing co-op just as the news came. During the pregnancy, we were living in a house with my partner L and his brother, J, and sharing cooking every night with a wider group of friends, including S's partner, M. I felt supported throughout and excited about the prospect of raising a child in community. I did not heavily involve my biological family in the pregnancy or birth so having my queer family around me made all the difference.

L came to all the scans with us. I did find it reassuring to have a romantic partner there, even though S was always present. It gave a different kind of support that I needed. We were planning a home birth in our living room with my whole household present. Luckily, my midwife thought our family arrangement was incredible and she took the time to get to know everyone. My best friend A (also J's partner) was going to be my main birth partner, which S was totally understanding about. A has always known how to keep me calm and S respected my choice entirely.

Sadly, towards the end of the pregnancy, I found out that I had obstetric cholestasis. Everything changed and became about endless hospital appointments, consultants, and blood tests. Eventually, I was taken into the hospital to be induced. I think I was the most visited person on the ward. There was always someone to go on walks around the hospital grounds with me, or to bring me snacks. The hospital staff struggled a lot more with the number of people in and out visiting me and seemed to find our family structure quite confusing. I felt the loss of the understanding midwife who had been with me throughout pregnancy so far.

When induction didn't work, I opted for a C-section. Being in the hospital had been a unpleasant experience, and I was keen for it to be over. A accompanied me into surgery, whilst my housemates made a phone tree for spreading news (including to my bio family), and designated between themselves people to wait in the hospital waiting room with S, others to come after the birth, etc. Unfortunately, I experienced a failure of the anesthetic and had a very traumatic birth experience. A was absolutely the best birth partner I could have had, including shouting at the surgeon when he was ignoring my screaming. I don't know how I could have coped without her there. It was scary for S and the others waiting, as they knew there had been complications, so I am glad they had each other at that time.

When I came round, S was there, and shortly after, when we were moved to the ward, every one of my queer family came. We have pictures of them all holding F the day he was born, which fill me with love whenever I look at them. After two days, we went home to start our strange new life.

At this stage L, J, S and I were living together with our two other co-op founders, M and C, coming round every day. We continued cooking for each other, which was an absolute godsend as a new parent. There were often people there to help with F, but S and I made it clear that we didn't want anyone to do more than they were happy to. F has always been solely our responsibility. Within a couple of months, two new friends joined our cooking group, and we became a family of nine.

The first two years of F's life are a haze of undiagnosed postnatal depression for me. I do not know how I would have gotten through them at all without this incredible family around me. S and I had already decided to loosely follow attachment parenting ideas, and I am incredibly grateful for that. Even through the times when I could hardly bear the idea of having a baby, I was still breastfeeding, co-sleeping, and exclusively slinging him. I think this helped a lot with us being able to form a bond and attachment with each other.

F wouldn't take a bottle of breastmilk, even if we tried, and I had trouble expressing, so our breastfeeding journey was intense. However, I'm glad we did manage to continue until he naturally weaned at the age of 3. The comfort of the sling meant everyone else could take F places too, which they did extensively. S has also always been an extremely committed coparent, dedicated to keeping us both doing 50% of the parenting as much as that can be managed. I have never once regretted my choice to have a baby with him rather than a donor.

As a group, we had a lot of tough times when F was screaming the house down, or I was so exhausted that I became an irritable person to live with, but somehow, we continued with the work of setting up the co-op. This culminated in us buying a house when F was 18 months old. At this point, M had moved away, but our family of eight now had an eight-bedroom house together that we owned and could improve. It was the most incredible feeling. For many of us for whom biological family is a difficult subject, I think the co-op provided a level of stability and the mutual support that had been missing from our lives.

I feel like having a wider network of adults involved in F's life has given him a tremendous sense of safety. Even when C moved out, F handled it brilliantly. After all, there were still lots of people around. A new housemate, D, moved in, and they became fast friends. When S made the decision to move out, F struggled a lot more, but his emotions were given space by a group of adults he had known since birth, and he adjusted.

Throughout F's life, S and I have had an amicable and cooperative relationship, and I truly believe this has been easier because we haven't had the romantic element to deal with. F gets to see his parents in fulfilling romantic relationships, just not with each other. Because of this, he has a lot of close, important adult figures in his life to listen and advocate for him if S and I are struggling with anything. I think that is an incredible gift for a child, and not one that any of us feel we had in our childhood.

S and I have had some difficult patches in our relationship, but after a period of living further away, he now lives only ten minutes from the co-op. Our tribe just doesn't fit in one house anymore. The co-op now has two houses, and we have a lot of other queer households nearby that we consider family. In fact, we seem to be attracting queer friends to our town now, which delights me.

As soon as I reached my teenage years, I thought of having a family. My vision evolved from finding a way to have a baby via donor with a monogamous girlfriend to the set-up I have today, which is something I could never have envisaged. But all along, I have been focused on the important parts of what good family is: support, love, commitment, and honesty. I believe that is why I have the beautiful queer family I have today."

Conclusion

To sum up, you have a lot to consider and to decide before you begin making your family. Of course, all this thinking and discussing doesn't end when your baby arrives, but then, many folks enjoy pondering and conscientiously making decisions, and feel it makes them better parents and people.

It's useful to remember that plans don't always work out as you intended, so sometimes being flexible and seeing how you can make the best of a situation is necessary. Also, you don't have to stick to just one method of family creation or one way of living. For example, you can have one biological child and one adopted child, or one child with a known donor and another with an unknown one, and you can start your parenting journey as one flavor of LGBTQ+ and continue it as another. Things constantly change in life, and that includes you. So, think it all through, but don't stop yourself from doing something just because you're not sure what the absolutely most perfect choice is. After all, nothing is perfect in life. Sometimes we just do the best we can with the information and resources we have at the time.

Antenatal, Natal, and Postnatal

Pregnancy and Birth

Once you get pregnant and/or are expecting a child through a surrogate, governmental agency, or an adoption agency, you need to prepare for what comes next. For many people, this might mean attending classes, whether ones run by the health service, doctors/midwives, or adoption agency, or privately offered ones, while other folks will want to get busy planning who is going to be involved in the baby's arrival, and some might want to get shopping for clothes and equipment, and still others might just bury their heads in the sand and not think about it all too much. So, in this chapter, I'll talk about a few things you might want to consider before your baby or child's arrival and how it relates to being LGBTQ+.

Antenatal Education

If you're pregnant, you may wish to attend antenatal classes. Similarly, if you are planning to foster or adopt, you may want—or be required—to take certain preparatory classes. Some classes are online, some are in person, and some are a mix. One of the benefits to such courses is that you may meet other expecting parents in your local area. It can be nice to have a few new acquaintances who are going through the same stages as you at about the same time ("Is this normal?" is one of the most common questions parents seem to ask.[6]). These preparatory classes may be highly elucidating for you; you may learn lots about birth or parenting that you never knew before. You may also be someone who loves to read and learn, so much of it might be familiar already. Or, like most people, you may be somewhere in the middle, enjoying some of the material, and finding other bits rather dry or repetitive.

What is generally true, though, is that these classes tend not to be particularly LGBTQ+-oriented. I've lost track of the number of people who've told me they've attended a class where the instructor

---

6 Remember, there's a wide range of normal!

always talked about "moms and dads" or divided people into teams based on gender or presumed role, even when LGBTQ+ people in the class have kindly requested that things be done differently. It seems difficult for some instructors to be inclusive or to shift their language slightly. The onus shouldn't be on you to have to ask that the instructor say "parents" or that they don't make jokes about how dads just don't know how to change a diaper/nappy. Hilarious, isn't it?

So, what can you do? Well, if you want to take classes, you can ask queer or queer-friendly folks that you know for recommendations. You can look at information or reviews online. You can also ask to talk to the instructor beforehand, so you can explain your family and ask whether they can be mindful of it. If you do experience something unpleasant or exclusive, you can always make a complaint or ask for a refund, although that can be hard to do, especially at a time when you're already feeling vulnerable.

You might also choose to educate yourself through reading rather than, or in addition to, a course. While there are many websites about parenting, it's often harder to sort through what is fact-based online. Usually, governmental websites and the World Health Organization are dependable sources. In terms of books, look for ones that are research-based, which means that the authors are doctors, professors, journalists, or other experts who have read through academic research in order to understand what is accepted as true based on research rather than simply opinion. They might well have opinions of their own, but their work should not be biased. In the U.S., Praeclarus Press publishes such books and, in the UK, Pinter and Martin does so (these two publishers' books are available in both countries, as well as elsewhere). Even reputable publishers do publish books that aren't fully inclusive, unfortunately, so choose carefully. See Appendix 6 for some reading suggestions.

As a rule of thumb, listen to what people tell you, whether it's in a book or a class, or during a chat at the grocery store, and then think about what makes the most sense, given that we are mammals who have evolved to behave and parent in particular ways, and also ponder what has the strongest basis in research and knowledge about human development. Also consider what feels right for you and suits your thinking about parenthood. Ultimately, you need to follow your own instincts and decide what works best for you and your family, while keeping you all safe and healthy.

Which People?

Besides authors and course instructors, you may come across a multitude of other people on your journey to parenthood. Which ones depend in part on how you are building your family and on where you live. In the UK, for example, you're more likely to work with midwives, while in the U.S., antenatal and labor care tends to be carried out by doctors, particularly obstetricians.

If you are pregnant, you most likely will have come across doctors, nurses, and other healthcare professionals, such as sonographers, at places such as a fertility clinic, the hospital, or your general practitioner's office. You are quite likely to work with midwives as well. There are even independent midwives that you could hire; these are people who have trained and qualified as midwives but have decided to work either outside of the health services or in addition to it.

A doula, like an independent midwife, works outside of the healthcare system and is someone you hire to provide emotional and practical support while pregnant, during labor, and/or in the postpartum period. The difference is that a doula is not medically trained. Since there tends to be a lack of continuity of care for pregnant people, it can be comforting and hugely beneficial to hire an independent midwife and/or doula, because these people will work for you and be on your side, giving you accurate information, and supporting you to make the choices that work best for you and your family (remember, I work as a doula, so I'm biased, but I think doulas can make a huge difference in terms of how your pregnancy and birth go). Doulas and independent midwives often offer a sliding scale of fees and some also provide services for free for those in need, so please do not let finances stop you from getting the help you require. Many of the people I have mentioned in this section will be involved in some way in your pregnancy and as you have the baby.

After you have given birth, in an ideal world, you will be offered help with getting your baby latched on, if you are planning to use your breasts or chest to feed your baby. However, postnatal wards and time constraints being what they are, you may find that you need to phone a breastfeeding helpline or attend a feeding group or café. There, you will likely come across peer supporters, breast-feeding/chestfeeding counselors, and/or lactation consultants. They all have different levels of knowledge, with an International Board-Certified Lactation Consultant (IBCLC) possessing the highest amount of training and certification. Some of these people volunteer their time, others charge, and many do a combination of both, depending on circumstances. As with pregnancy, if money is an issue, there is usually help to get free of charge or at a lower cost.

Regardless of whether you make your family through pregnancy, adoption, or in other ways, you may also need to work with social workers, therapists/counselors, governmental or private agencies, and/or lawyers. In regard to lawyers, you will probably want to have a will, clarifying what will happen to you, your estate, and your children if you pass away. Some of these professionals may be assigned to you, whereas you might be able to choose who you would prefer to work with in other cases. If you do have the freedom to choose, do your research. Ask others for recommendations, look on the internet, and read books to get ideas about which people you might want. It is acceptable, and quite sensible, to interview a range of doulas or lawyers or whomever before deciding who you relate to best and would prefer to work with. You will likely want to ask them about the services they offer, their experience, LGBTQ+-friendliness and knowledge, costs, and potential approach to your specific journey.

All professionals will understand if you decide to work with someone else and they will all have had that happen before, so if you do choose someone else, politely thank those you won't be hiring and wish them well. Don't just leave them wondering whether you'll be getting back in touch or not. On that note, be aware that they can also refuse to work with you for any reason. They might have a personal conflict that they don't tell you about or they might decide that they aren't the best people to provide you with high-quality service. They should not refuse to work with you due to your gender and/or sexuality, but if they are prejudiced or uncomfortable, they should acknowledge that they aren't the best match for you.

As you are embarking on your family creation journey, in other words, start considering what professionals you want or need to involve and what traits or skills you want them to have. Take your time and try to find the people who best fit your budget, timeframe, and particular situation.

Baby or Child Loss

I'm sorry, but it's important to pause for a moment and to talk about baby or child loss. This is a real issue; one we don't talk enough about. Baby or child loss here refers to a range of sad experiences: abortion, chemical pregnancy, miscarriage, stillbirth, death from illness, or a foster placement or adoption falling through. Since this book is focused on the early years, this generally means the loss of a fetus, baby, or young child up until a couple of years old, but certainly children can, unfortunately, die or otherwise be lost to you beyond that stage too.

Abortion

It may be that you get pregnant, but the time isn't right for you to have a baby, or you may decide that this particular fetus isn't one you are able to carry to term, such as if health issues have been detected that would mean that the baby would be severely unwell or even unlikely to survive once born, or if the fetus was conceived through rape or an unhealthy relationship. This is a controversial subject and while abortion is not allowed in some places, it is absolutely your body, and it should be your choice whether to continue with the pregnancy. Even if you choose to abort the fetus and feel comfortable with this decision, you may find that you still think about the fetus or wonder what might have been, or perhaps you might notice that some of your friends or relatives are less than supportive about your choice. Be sure to get help as needed, physically and emotionally, when going through an abortion.

Chemical Pregnancy

A chemical pregnancy is an early miscarriage, usually in the first few weeks of the pregnancy. If you are consciously trying for a baby, you are probably hyperaware of your body and you might also be taking pregnancy tests earlier than some other people, who might not think to do so until they've missed a period. So, while some folks won't recognize they were ever pregnant and have had a chemical pregnancy, those of us who are undergoing fertility treatment or who are tracking our cycles will know. Whether it's a chemical pregnancy or a later miscarriage, it can be incredibly painful to experience the loss of a wanted baby.

Miscarriage

A miscarriage is the loss of a pregnancy up until about the 20th (or 24th, depending on where you live) week of gestation. We're too secretive about miscarriage in our society, believing that we shouldn't even announce pregnancy until it's at least 12 weeks in, as though there's something shameful about an early pregnancy or about losing a baby. Personally, I think we'd be better off talking openly about these things, because miscarriages are thought to happen in 25% of pregnancies (King, 2020), sometimes because there is something wrong with the fetus, so the body aborts it, and sometimes for no clear reason at all. If you look at the people you know, around one in every four will experience a miscarriage, or will be going through that right now, potentially without feeling like they can talk about it. As Kay King writes, "It doesn't feel like that many, because they pass us by in secret…we do need to feel able to share our stories of loss if we need support to recover" (2020, p. 45).

Stillbirth

A stillbirth—when a baby is born dead—is generally defined as happening during the second half of the pregnancy, when others usually are aware that you are pregnant. The stillbirth might happen because of birth defects or because of placental failure or for a variety of other reasons, most out of your control. It's thought that around 0.5% of pregnancies end in a stillbirth. Sometimes you will know the baby has died, because you will stop feeling movements and an ultrasound will show that the heartbeat has stopped. Sometimes you may not know the baby has died until the baby has come out. You will still have to birth the baby, whether vaginally or via a C-section. Nowadays, parents of babies born dead will have the chance to cuddle their baby, change their baby's clothes, and to take photos or even hand and footprints of the baby. There are also cooling pads that can be placed in a cot or crib, which will preserve the body a little longer so the parents and older siblings can have some more time with the child to say goodbye.

All of the forms of loss mentioned so far—abortion, chemical pregnancy, miscarriage, and stillbirth—relate to the death of a fetus or baby during pregnancy, when you or your partner will physically experience the presence and then the absence of the baby. You may or may not choose to try for another pregnancy again. You will, no matter what, need time to grieve and support from those around you.

Loss of Fostering or Adoptive Placement

It is also possible to experience the loss of a baby or child when a fostering or adoption placement falls through. You may have received photos or even met and gotten to know the child you were going to foster or adopt. You might have even had the child living with you and then found out that they were going to be returned to their biological parents or other relatives, or were going to be moved to another placement. It might also be the case that you had planned to adopt and then realized that this situation was not right for you or for the child. Whatever happens, losing a child this way is also anguishing. In this situation, you may understandably be worried about trying to foster or adopt again. Be sure to talk to the agencies or social workers that are involved and get their input and help, so you can move forward in a way that feels right for you.

Accident or Illness

Finally, a child might die in an accident or through illness. I don't have the scope here to talk through all the ways that this might occur, but it is, sadly, more common than we think. Although childhood mortality rates have improved greatly in recent times, the World Health Organization estimates that over five million children under 5 died in 2019, with primary reasons being:

> preterm birth complications, birth asphyxia/trauma, pneumonia, congenital anomalies, diarrhoea and malaria, all of which can be prevented or treated with access to simple, affordable interventions including immunization, adequate nutrition, safe water and food and quality care by a trained health provider when needed (World Health Organization, 2020).

Clearly, we all need to do better to take care of the children of the world, because so many of these causes could be prevented. This does not mean, of course, that you are to blame if your child passes away.

No matter how it happens, the loss of a baby or child is a source of harrowing grief that is likely to last for a long time, quite possibly the rest of your days. It is essential that you allow yourself to grieve in whatever way feels right for you. All your feelings are valid. You may want and need to talk to others, such as therapists or friends or support groups, about what you are going through, and you may need to take some time off work or time out from your usual activities. You likely will eventually come to some decisions about how to go forward on your parenting journey. However you want to move on, be sure you make the decision that feels right for you. Most importantly, be gentle with yourself. This is sure to be one of the hardest things you'll ever experience.

A Story about Baby Loss

Rebecca and Jules, a lesbian couple, have experienced baby loss. Rebecca writes:

"My wife Jules and I have a wonderful daughter, who is 4. But it was a long road to get where we are today.

We started trying for a baby in 2014 and were lucky enough to fall pregnant quickly. Unfortunately, we lost the baby. Shortly after, we lost another. Losing babies is a pain like no other; it rocks your world.

We tried a third time, now using IVF, and thankfully, it worked the first time and 9 months later, our little girl, Evie, was born.

Since that wonderful experience we have gone on to try four more times. Sadly, each attempt ended in heartbreak for us. Thankfully we have our little girl and Evie is the most amazing little person *ever* and makes her Mummy and Mama proud every single day. But we will never forget our six other babies and our lives will be forever changed due to the losses."

Trauma

As an LGBTQ+ person, you are likely to have experienced some difficult things in your life. Okay, you might be one of the lucky ones, someone who was always loved and accepted by everyone around you, someone whose life has turned out as they hoped, and if so, I'm happy for you. Well, happy and a tiny bit envious.

But most of us have had some struggles. Maybe you were rejected by relatives, kicked out, or cut off. Perhaps friends, or even partners, gasped with shock and were disgusted when you came out. You might have had to deal with homophobia, biphobia, transphobia, or generalized queerphobia, whether from friends, relatives, colleagues, or society at large. It could be that you have spent time in anti-queer environments, or have been forced into conversion therapy that tried to make you change who you were. You may have been harassed or bullied. You could have been subjected to corrective rape, where someone tried to forcibly change your sexuality or gender. Or perhaps you've experienced other forms of queer hatred and violence.

It could also be the case that during this pregnancy or a previous one, you have found yourself the subject of ridicule, or you've been misgendered, or your relationship with your partner hasn't been recognized. Maybe you've corrected people, but you're tired of the burden always being placed on you.

You understandably might be feeling sad, angry, weary, traumatized, frightened, or any other emotions. All your experiences and feelings are valid. It's difficult to move past these sorts of things. They shape us and can make us feel unsafe and scared. If you've been through anything like this, I'm sorry. I'd love for you to be getting support. So, if you feel it would be helpful, look for a charity that can provide guidance, links, book suggestions, a peer supporter, or a forum. Maybe contact a queer-friendly therapist and see if counseling will help (many therapists have a sliding scale of fees, so ask if you need to). If appropriate, perhaps contact a lawyer or the police about bringing a case against anyone who assaulted you. Talk things through with your partner or with someone like a doula or midwife, to see how they can best help you during your pregnancy and labor, or during the adoption process. It can be difficult to move forward with your life and to transition to parenthood when you've been through something so hard. There's no shame in getting help.

Take good care of yourself and be kind to yourself. Life is tough. Don't make it harder by beating yourself up about experiences that were out of your control.

Birth Preferences

Okay, let's take a break from these painful subjects. Assuming that you are pregnant and due to give birth, you will need to consider how, where, and with what people present. You have more control over this than many people assume. Midwives and doctors may advise you to do something in particular, and friends or relatives might tell you what they did and what they think you should do, but ultimately, it is your choice. If there is a medical emergency, of course, you may not have as many choices, but in general, you should have quite a lot of input into what will certainly be one of the most transformative experiences in your life.

It's true that you can't plan exactly what will happen during a labor and birth, but you can consider what you think would work best for you, and try to ensure that this happens, to whatever extent possible. It's wise to spend time pondering this, both on your own and with your partner or whoever will accompany you during birth, so you can write up a list of preferences. This will be beneficial to your midwives, doctors, doula, and birth partner, because they can refer to it during your labor, doing their utmost to help you achieve the birth you want, as there will be times when you're not quite in the mood to have a chat about it. The last thing you want when you're experiencing surges, for example, is for someone to pop up in front of you and say, "So, how many candles did you want me to light?" In an ideal world, people would just check over your preferences document and try to fulfil your wishes.

So, what kinds of items should you note on your document? This can range hugely, depending on what matters to you. For instance, you may want certain people with you, perhaps your partner, or a friend, or a doula, or the parents of the baby if you're a surrogate, while you'd like others to stay out, such as that particularly annoying

relative who just doesn't ever stop talking. You might have a preference about whether student midwives are present or not. You could
have opinions about what sort of language people use around you;
this could include your own pronouns or terms ("Please use my first
name rather than calling me 'Mom'"), or about the language of birth,
such as asking them to say "surges" rather than "contractions."

You might recognize that you feel safest at home or, on the
contrary, that you'd like to be in a more clinical setting, with access
to medications. You might also feel that you'd prefer to start off
in one location and then move to another, or you might not care
about that at all. (More on different locations below.) You're likely
to have opinions about which medications you'd like (none, all, or
something in between) and which tools or approaches you'd prefer,
such as a pool for a water birth or the use of forceps.

Methods of Pain Relief

METHOD	EXPLANATION
Hypnobirthing/visualization/ relaxation	This focuses your attention away from the pain (or, some- times, onto the pain).
Breathing	Focusing on your breath can relax you and help keep you from panicking.
Massage	Someone rubs your back (or other sore body part) to release tension and pain.
TENS machine (transcutaneous electrical nerve stimulation)	You stick the machine to you, and it provides some electrical current, which can distract you or make you feel the pain less.
Water	Warm water in a shower, bath, or birthing pool is known to be soothing and relaxing.

Being active	Changing positions, walking, and moving around can make you more comfortable.
Complementary medicine	Some people find acupuncture, homeopathy, reflexology, and so on helpful.
Gas and air (oxygen and nitrous oxide)	A drug that decreases your awareness of pain.
Pethidine	Another drug to relax you.
Epidural	Local anesthetic that numbs you.
General anesthetic	When you're put completely under, so you aren't aware of what's happening. (This may be necessary in an emergency or if you have anxiety about birth.)

You may want to be wearing a particular, favored item of clothing or jewelry as you birth your baby. You could be someone who wants the room they birth in to look or feel a specific way, with photographs, artwork on the walls, incense burning, candles glowing, or music playing. You may have a list of snacks that you know will give you energy as you labor, and so on. As you can tell, there are a lot of possible things to think about, ranging from quite large decisions (such as whether to have pain medication) to potentially smaller ones (such as what brand of chocolate bars to have on hand).

Once your baby is born, you'll have even more decisions to make. If all is well, the best thing will be for you to get at least one golden hour of skin-to-skin contact with your baby before anyone starts weighing, measuring, checking you over, trying to move you to another room or ward, offering you a shower, or anything else. In that golden hour, you'll want to stare at this amazing creature you brought forth and you most likely want to get the baby latched on to you for colostrum, unless you are certain you want to formula-feed (more on feeding below). For a surrogate, the parents of the baby may want to be the first ones to hold the baby instead of the person who gestated them. You will need to make your wishes known about how you'd like to birth the placenta (with the help of an injection or not), who is going to cut the umbilical cord, whether you want someone to make an announcement about your baby's body parts (in other words, if you want commentary on your baby's genitals/sex), if you want to give your baby vitamin K (and, if so, if you want the injection or an oral vitamin), and so forth.

Since you probably won't be up for thinking through all this while actively in the throes of labor and birth, you might want to do the research and pondering while pregnant. Remember, you can change your document or your wishes at any point, and you do also have to go with your body and your circumstances. Having some idea in advance about what might suit you best will save you worry later. See Appendix 3 for a list of things topics to consider while you are writing up your birth preferences and Appendix 4 for a suggestion of items to include in your bag, if you're planning on giving birth in a hospital or birth center.

Home Birth

As you're thinking through your birth preferences, one of the biggest things to decide is where you'd like to have your baby. Your main choices here are a home birth or a hospital birth.

I have a feeling you aren't going to be surprised when I say that a home birth is, well, giving birth at home. This could be your own home or someone else's (as long as they give you permission, of course). Research shows that homebirths are generally as safe as, and sometimes safer than, hospital births.. For people who have already had one or more straightforward births, a home birth is usually quite a low-risk option. The Birthplace Study run by the University of Oxford comments that:

> For women having a second or subsequent baby, home
> births and midwifery unit births appear to be safe for the
> baby and offer benefits for the mother ... For multiparous

women, birth in a non-obstetric unit setting significantly and substantially reduced the odds of having an intra-partum caesarean section, instrumental delivery or episiotomy (Oxford Population Health, 2020).

We should add that these stats are true for men and other people giving birth too. On the other hand, for a first-time parent:

there were 9.3 adverse perinatal outcome events per 1000 planned home births compared with 5.3 per 1000 births for births planned in obstetric units, and this finding was statistically significant (Oxford Population Health, 2020).

In other words, current research shows that for a first-time parent, it might be safer to give birth in a birth center or hospital, whereas for those giving birth the second or third time, being at home offers advantages, such as a lower likelihood of interventions. You will have to decide for yourself how you feel about the statistics. You might, for instance, decide to start at home and then transfer to the hospital later, if you want or need to.

Mammals need to feel safe to give birth. From an evolutionary perspective, if we had a predator after us and we stopped to have a baby, both the birthing parent and the new baby would quickly become a nice meal. So we are primed to want to be somewhere safe. Nighttime tends to be safer, with more animals asleep, which is why more people go into labor or give birth in the dark. Based on that, it makes sense that for some of us, staying at home to have our baby is the preferred choice, because it feels safest and coziest. You won't have to worry about when the right time is to go to the hospital, or if the hospital room will have a birth ball, or whether your labor will slow under the bright hospital lights. You can stay where you are, in your own little nest.

Not everyone feels safe in their home, of course, and if you don't, you might want to think about that as an issue in your life more broadly. You might also feel that your home doesn't have the space for you to pace around or put down a birth pool or that you don't want to get blood and amniotic fluid on your things. It's absolutely your right to decide that a home birth isn't for you.

If you do want a home birth, there are some other things to consider. For instance, you'll want to think about what sort of set-up you want. Do you need to hire a birthing pool? Will you want a birth ball or birth stool? Do you need some plastic sheeting to protect your sofa, bed, or carpeting? Will you want to hang a rope or some towels over a door so you can hang off of them during labor? You can decide how you want the space to look, sound, and smell. You might like to light candles or incense or an aromatherapy oil diffuser. There could be particular photos or artworks you'd like around. You might tape some affirmations up around the house or perhaps play some special music. You'll be free to decorate your space in the way you'd like best.

Medicine is another big point during labor. At home, you won't have access to an epidural. Some midwives will bring gas and air over, but they often leave it in the car unless you request it. So, you'll need to consider whether you should have a stash of acetaminophen/paracetamol on hand, or if you'll want to get a TENS machine (transcutaneous electrical nerve stimulation), or whether you'd prefer to use the warmth of your shower, bath, or birthing pool. You may choose to take a hypnobirthing course while pregnant and to focus on visualizations and breathing as your methods for pain relief. Do read up on the methods and any possible side effects before deciding.

If you have any older children, you might want to include them in the birth if you're at home. They might be able to encourage you, or give you cuddles, or they might just be excited to see a baby being born. On the other hand, you might feel that you'd prefer them to be occupied so you can focus on the baby. If so, you'll want to arrange for them to go elsewhere or for a relative, friend, or babysitter to come to your place so they can care for the kids.

Who will you want to be there more generally? It's your house, so you can have as many or as few people there as you like. Perhaps you just want it to be you and the midwife. Maybe you want your partner, a friend, or a relative. You might want to have a doula. In some cultures, it's common to have a range of folks there to support the birthing person and to welcome the new baby. You might like that, or you might prefer to have different people at different stages. You can also change your mind during labor and invite more people or ask some to leave. Your home should be your sanctuary during labor, so think carefully in advance about who and what makes you feel safe.

On a practical note, don't forget your pets. I've been to a couple of births where dogs have been running around. Some people find it comforting to hug and pet their dog, while others need to send the dog outside or to stay with a neighbor. Make arrangements in advance and be sure to provide pet food so your animal doesn't go hungry.

Some people think they'd like a home birth but then worry that something might go wrong. As I noted above, home birth is generally safe. But still, we all get anxious about anything happening to ourselves or our babies. For this reason, I recommend calculating where your nearest hospital is and how long it could take you to get there from home at different times of the day, such as in the middle of the night or at rush hour. Depending on where you live, it might be an easy matter for an ambulance to come get you and transfer you to the hospital if needed. Much of labor happens a lot more slowly than people imagine based on the films and TV shows they've seen, which means you generally would have the time to get to the hospital for a different level of help.

Having a home birth usually means you have more control over the setting and the people involved, which is something that some folks like and want. If you think you'd be most comfortable in your own bed, lights turned low, your favorite music playing, treating birth like a natural event rather than a medicalized one, then a home birth might be for you.

Pros and Cons of a Home Birth

PROS	CONS
You're in your own home and everything feels safe and familiar.	There will probably be some mess to clean up and you may want to protect some of your furniture or other belongings.
You aren't likely to be pressured to take drugs.	You won't have access to many drugs, if you decide you want them. Gas and air is usually available.
You're less likely to need interventions.	You will have to buy or rent your own birth pool, if you want to labor in one.
You won't have to leave your older children, if you have any, though you might need to arrange some care for them.	You may want or need to go into the hospital, depending on how your labor and delivery progress.
You may have more continuity of care.	There are some situations where a home birth is considered risky or inappropriate, although it is still your choice.

A Story About Home Birth

We have previously heard from Perse and Deb, a lesbian couple now in New Zealand. Deb gave birth to their two younger children at home. Here, she writes about what that process was like and how her family was treated during their home births:

"My maternity care in Aotearoa New Zealand was provided by community-based midwives, known as Lead Maternity Carers (LMCs). LMCs are funded by the government, but effectively operate as private providers—women and other pregnant people choose their preferred LMC from a dating-type website where all local providers have their profiles. On both occasions, my LMCs were lovely and caring women (I chose a different LMC for my second pregnancy, as I planned on a home birth), and the fact that we were a lesbian couple didn't seem to faze them or affect their professional interactions with us or the clinical care they provided. I had already met my second LMC during my time working on the obstetric wards at the local hospital, when I worked there as a junior doctor.

I birthed both my babies at home, although the first time was completely unplanned, as our intention had always been to go to the birthing center we had chosen. On that occasion, I was attended by two midwives—colleagues of my LMC who was in theatre with another laboring woman and was unable to attend us urgently. I had, therefore, not met either of the midwives, but they were lovely, and showed no surprise or discomfort around us, which meant I could concentrate fully on the job at hand. They took some beautiful photos of us on our phones in the minutes after our son was born, which was such a thoughtful and caring thing to do for us, when we were so full of adrenaline, relief, and exhaustion.

After my first delivery, my son and I were ambulanced into hospital so I could get my deep tear surgically repaired. When I came out of theatre, our baby had developed breathing difficulties due to his rapid passage into the world and retained water on his lungs. He was admitted to the Neonatal Intensive Care Unit (NICU), and I was admitted to the maternity ward. Again, my experience was colored more by having worked alongside my own and my son's health providers (both doctors and nurses), in obstetrics and on NICU, than by my same-sex relationship. My lesbian identity was well-known, as was my pregnancy and impending birth when I had gone on maternity leave a few weeks prior. I suspect that the other people on the ward wondered why "the lesbians" got so many social visits from clinical staff.

My second delivery was a planned home birth, and my LMC was thankfully able to attend. As is also the case in the UK, she was accompanied by a second midwife, whom I hadn't met before. My LMC specifically chose her second on the basis of her knowledge of us as a couple, and her assessment of a good fit between us, which proved to be the case. They took amazing care of me, making themselves familiar with our kitchen so they could provide me and my wife with hot and cold drinks, could keep the birthing pool topped-up with hot water, and could ensure that the atmosphere in the spare room (where I gave birth) was peaceful, calm, and filled with aroha (love).

Again, our midwives captured the final moments before I gave birth, and the first hour or so afterwards on our phones and took exceptional care of me in the hours after my birth-giving when my placenta refused to detach, and I suffered heavy blood loss. Being familiar with my profession, they calmly talked me through each procedure, which included a couple of interventions designed to stem my blood loss, a fluid transfusion to stabilize my blood pressure, and the suturing of my tear. Nothing fazed them, they communicated honestly and openly, being clear on the point at which they would make the decision to transfer me to the hospital if necessary, and they made us feel seen and totally accepted as the lesbian parents of our wonderful new daughter."

Hospital Birth or Birth Center

The other main choice for birth is for it to take place not at your home, which to many people means the hospital. But it's important to note that there are options within this.

For example, there are birth centers, which tend to be more like the cozy atmosphere at home, but with slightly more medical equipment and medical professionals available. Then, within the hospital itself, depending on where you live, you can be in a midwife-led unit or a consultant-led ward. Midwives and doctors at the hospitals tend to try to make the midwife-led ward more like a birth center, in that they aim for a "home away from home" atmosphere, with soft lighting and birthing pools. Usually, you have access to more drugs, such as pethidine, at a birth center or midwife-led unit, than you would at home, but you are still encouraged to use a TENS machine, visualizations, or water to manage the pain.

If you want or need more interventions, you can choose the consultant-led/obstetrician-led unit. Just remember the concept of the cascade of interventions; this is where one intervention is likely to lead to another. Interventions can include the use of forceps or ventouse/vacuum cup (to help pull the baby out), an episiotomy (a cut to your perineum), more medications (such as an epidural), or a Cesarean section. You may also need surgical repair after birth, if you have torn the skin and muscle in the perineum. There are different grades of tears, and some require stitching, either by a midwife or in an operating room, while others are considered just grazes.

A Cesarean, or C-section, is where an incision is made, and the baby is pulled out of your abdomen rather than coming through the vaginal canal. A C-section can be an emergency or planned and there are a variety of reasons for either option. In an emergency, it might be that the baby is getting distressed during labor, or you are getting exhausted, so you decide you'd like to opt for a section In a planned scenario, you might know that the baby will need urgent medical care immediately after birth, so you want to be in the hospital. Therefore, scheduling it is sensible. Another situation might be if the baby is thought to be large (though ultrasounds are often considered unreliable[7]) or if the baby is in a position that would make birth challenging. If you have a C-section, you can usually ask for it to be gentle, where the lights are low, the music is calm, and the baby is placed on your chest immediately. You can also request that some bacteria from your vaginal canal be taken and smeared on the baby after birth, since now we know a lot about how important bacteria is for the microbiome (Harman & Wakeford, 2016; Reardon, 2019).

You will generally need a longer recovery time after birth if you have had a major intervention, such as forceps or a C-section, or if you have had surgical repair due to a tear. You may not be able to drive for 6 or so weeks, so be sure to accept that and to arrange plenty of help (and chauffeurs) for that period of time.

You also need to remember that the number of birth partners at a hospital is usually limited, most often to just one or two, so you might not be able to have all the people you hoped to while in labor. On the other hand, some are glad for the hospital's strict rules, since it gives them an excuse to bar people they don't want to offend but equally don't actually want around. Hospitals also tend to have limited visiting times, which you may or may not like. You may end up alone in a hospital bed with a new baby for many hours without your partner or anyone else, and this could feel hard for you. You might appreciate some time on your own, just getting to know your new baby without loads of people demanding a cuddle.

Some people like the medicalized atmosphere of the hospital. They find it comforting to know that all the help they need is at hand. Others appreciate knowing that there are multiple people

---

7 Many popular articles suggest that ultrasounds are 10% to 15% off, or can be plus or minus one pound, which is quite a lot when you're talking about a baby who is usually somewhere between five and eight pounds. Recent scholarly research notes that this variation depends on the number of weeks of gestation when an ultrasound is performed, the formulae used by the sonographer, which measurements are taken, and so on. Julia Milner and Jane Arezina (2018) write that, "During the last decade, accuracy of ultrasound calculation of EFW [estimated fetal weight] appears to have increased, with recent studies consistently producing random errors below 10%." Still, 10% might be considered quite a large number when it comes to errors, so you will have to decide whether to trust the figures you're given after an ultrasound.

giving birth and recovering at the same time. Depending on the set-up of the ward, you might even get to meet and chat with other new parents. Some birthing parents even like the hospital food! So, whether you need more medical help or whether you just appreciate being in the birth center or hospital unit, giving birth in the hospital might be the right thing for you.

Pros and Cons of a Hospital Birth

PROS	CONS
You'll have access to all the drugs you might need.	Hospitals are quite busy, so staff might not always be able to come with the drugs as quickly as you'd like.
Some hospitals try for a "home away from home" experience.	A hospital is not your home, no matter how hard they try.
If you need interventions, hospitals are the place to have them.	Some doctors are a bit too eager to provide interventions, which you may or may not need. Also, one intervention might lead to another.
There are more staff around to help you.	You might find the busyness overwhelming.
The number of birth partners or visitors might be limited.	The number of birth partners or visitors might be limited.

A Story About a Planned C-Section

Rebecca, a lesbian, had a planned C-section. She describes her situation:

"During my pregnancy, it was discovered that the baby was in the breech position, something that I tried to change in many ways including yoga, swimming, and lying upside down. I was offered the ECV (external cephalic version)[8] but after looking into it, I decided it wasn't for us.

So, a C-section was the only safe way to go! A C-section was the one thing I never wanted, but I wanted my baby to be delivered safely, so I got my head around it all and we had a planned C-section.

My wife, Jules, was with me the whole time and it was actually a nice, relaxed atmosphere. Obviously, you can't feel anything during the procedure and it's all done quickly. The baby is out in around 10 minutes.

Our baby, Evie, went straight to Jules when she was out. I always wanted her to anyway but obviously, with a C-section, you don't have much choice, as your arms are on your chest and full of catheters. It was so lovely for Jules to have that first cuddle. Hearing those wonderful little cries was the best sound I think either of us had ever heard.

The whole time we were in hospital we were never treated any differently for being a same-sex couple. My only grumble throughout the process was the fact the donor kept being referred to as "the dad," something he is not, nor ever will be. Obviously, we corrected them and hopefully in the last four years, the language used in those situations has changed."

---

8 External cephalic version is a maneuver where they try to turn a baby so that it is facing downwards. The doctor will move the baby from the outside (i.e., by pushing on your stomach). This may cause some discomfort.

A Stor, About a Positive Hospital Birth

Emily, a bisexual woman, has had three positive hospital births. She used hypnobirthing techniques and felt well-supported but did experience bi-erasure. She writes:

"I had planned a home birth for my first child but ended up being induced in the hospital. This was a positive experience, so I chose a hospital birth for my second and third children too.

For my second birth, I went into labor naturally, so I was able to be on the midwife-led unit and have a water birth like I wanted.

I used my natal hypnotherapy CDs (a form of hypnobirthing) to help me manage the labor and was able to give birth in the birth pool using only gas and air.

As a bisexual woman who was in a heterosexual relationship, my queerness felt pretty much erased throughout the duration of that relationship, and definitely during pregnancy, labor, and early childhood settings. I was always assumed to be straight, I believe.

I am definitely happy with my decision to have hospital births. There were a few negatives, such as a rude midwife who made the experience difficult and a lack of help and support. If I had been able to be more assertive (or had a birth partner who was awake and able to advocate for me), it would have negated a lot of the issues.

But I also felt so empowered doing it alone. The hours I had spent preparing with my CDs at home and doing pregnancy yoga paid off. I felt like a strong fertility goddess.

I would also say, if you know you're in labor, trust your body. Because I was calm due to the hypnobirthing, the midwives did not believe I was in active labor, and this was upsetting and made me doubt myself. If this wasn't labor, how was I going to be able to manage when I was in actual labor? I would have been much more relaxed if I had trusted my body and tuned out their doubts.

My third child was breech until partway through the pregnancy, when I underwent an ECV (External Cephalic Version) procedure, where a doctor turned the fetus the right way round from the outside.

Due to the ECV procedure, I was slightly higher risk, and it was recommended that I give birth in the hospital. I went into labor at home and went to the hospital later that day. I knew I would be safe if any problems did arise.

As a labor experience, it was probably the most painful out of my three labors and lasted 16.5 hours. So much for third babies being quick and easy! But I was supported by excellent staff, and an ex-partner who managed to put aside our recent separation and the tension to be fully supportive and present for me. When the baby found it difficult to breathe in her first few moments of life, the neonatal team were on hand straight away to assist and take care of her. I was happy with my decision

Being bisexual in a heterosexual relationship, I don't feel like my sexuality entered into the equation during my pregnancy or labor, which is a common experience, as bi-erasure is prevalent."

Free Birth

Depending on your situation, you might feel that you want to give birth without medical staff or other professionals around you. This is what is usually called a free birth or unassisted birth.

Sometimes this happens accidentally, such as if you're aiming to give birth at home and the baby arrives before the midwife. Other times, this is planned. You may be someone who dislikes the medical establishment or even has had a traumatic experience with medical professionals, so you may feel more comfortable without them. You might have had a difficult previous birth. You might feel that there's a lack of continuity of care antenatally, and you don't feel confident in the medical practice, midwives, or doctors that are serving you. It could be that there are reasons why you are particularly keen to avoid a hospital or contact with other people at a specific time, such as during a pandemic. You could feel that as an LGBTQ+ person, you aren't likely to be treated as fairly as you have the right to expect in the hospital. Depending on where you live, you might want to avoid the high costs of giving birth in a hospital. You might simply want to keep this experience as something private just for you, or perhaps you and your partner, or you and a doula. It's your choice how you give birth.

If you decide to go for an unassisted birth, you may want to read up on labor and birth in detail beforehand, so you know what to expect. You may also choose to have some emergency supplies, or the number to the local hospital, or a friend on standby to drive you to the hospital, just in case, or you might feel you'd rather not consider those things.

There are a few situations where free birth might be risky, such as if you're expecting multiples, if the baby has known health problems, if you need extra support for mental or physical issues, and so on. But even so, it is up to you to decide how you want to give birth and what feels best for your situation.

Pros and Cons of a Free Birth

PROS	CONS
You can give birth where you like.	You won't easily have access to medications or interventions.
You can choose who will be with you.	Your chosen support people may not be available.
You will most likely be treated how you like and deserve to be.	This might be risky, depending on your particular situation.

Conclusion

Preparing to welcome your baby to the world is exciting and daunting. The more you are informed about it all beforehand, the more likely you are to make the decisions that are right for you. This could help you have an empowering experience that forever changes you as a person. Even if your antenatal period or birth doesn't turn out exactly as you would have liked, doing your research and considering all your options will help you throughout the process, because the words, concepts, and experiences will be familiar to you and, in an ideal world, you will feel able to advocate for yourself and your family.

You've Got a Child!

You've welcomed a child into your family! Congratulations! But, um, what next? In this section, I'll look at a range of topics, including recovering from birth, parental leave, transitioning to parenthood, and what to tell people.

Recovery

Regardless of how you birth your family—C-section, vaginal birth, adoption, marriage, etc.—you're going to need some time to recover and adjust.

This might be surprising news, though. Many advertisements and TV shows make birth and parenthood look so glamorous. You pop a baby out and then you're back to the same you, mentally and physically, that you were before, right?

Not really. No matter how you've become a family, you've likely been through something of a marathon. This may have included deep discussions, mountains of paperwork, blood tests, meetings with health and legal professionals, references from other people, medical procedures, medications, home visits, counseling, lots of cash, stress and worry, and, for some people, the enormous labor that is giving birth. You're probably exhausted and overwhelmed.

You need some time to recover from all that. I like the concept I've often heard of 2 weeks in bed, 2 weeks on the bed, and 2 weeks around the bed. What it means is that you spend 2 weeks resting in bed, sleeping and cuddling as much as you can. Then you spend 2 weeks hanging out on your bed, sitting up, reading, and chatting and 2 weeks taking it easy in your room or house. You don't have to take this literally and feel tied to the bed for those weeks. It's just a general idea about how you should take at least 2 weeks, and, ideally, a month or two, to treat yourself gently and not pressure yourself to get up and do all the things you were probably used to doing before birth.

Basically, don't overdo it. Imagine what you'd tell someone else in the same situation and then do the same things for yourself.

In an ideal world, for example, you wouldn't need to think about cooking. Maybe you could prepare and freeze extra meals before the arrival of your child, or perhaps other people could provide you with food, or you could use a grocery or meal delivery service. Similarly, don't worry about tidying your house or doing laundry. Of course, you need clean clothes at times (I'm not sure why, given how messy kids are and how messy they make us), but laundry shouldn't be your job just now. If you have given birth, your partner or friends or relatives can certainly put a load of washing on or vacuum the floors or manage whatever practical housekeeping tasks need to be done. Perhaps someone will give you the gift of some hours from a cleaning company or maid service.

What I'm suggesting here is that you let go of the usual everyday responsibilities around your house and allow other people to help you. Many of us aren't great at letting people do things for us, but if ever there were a time to accept offers of help, it's now.

While you're having this restful period in which to recover and get to know your new family member, you should be mindful of your physical and emotional wellbeing. It is common for parents to experience postnatal depression, regardless of whether they have actually given birth themselves. If you find that you're feeling particularly sad or negative, or if you are feeling like you might hurt yourself or someone else, it's important to speak up and get help. Don't be ashamed. Many people can relate to how you're feeling and have been there too. It could be that talking it through openly with others helps you, or you might want medication or therapy. Acknowledging it is the first step and while it's hard to do that, it's vital.

Some Signs of Postpartum Depression

You feel sad, low, worthless, anxious, or helpless.
You are tearful.
You feel like you might harm yourself, your baby, or someone else.
You struggle to sleep or to wake up.
You are eating too much or too little.
You have little energy.
You are not interested in life.
You feel angry or upset with your baby, other children, or partner.
You are having negative thoughts about yourself.
You don't feel you are bonding with your baby.

Consider whether there are other things you could do that would help you during this time, such as going for a massage, having a warm bath, eating something especially yummy, getting to the swimming pool for a few laps, meeting a group of like-minded people, or taking a nap. If it would be beneficial and safe to do, see if you can make it happen. I know this is easier said than done, but the truth is that you can't properly care for a baby or child if you aren't also being taken care of.

Once you've welcomed a child into your family, your life will not be the same. It's essential that you take time to adjust to your new reality and to recover from the process. You can't go back to the old you, so try to get to know this new version of you and be kind to that person.

Transitioning to Parenthood

When you've brought a child into your life, through whatever process you chose, you're probably going to start thinking about what parenthood means to you. You'll undoubtedly spend a lot of time pondering what sort of parent you want to be and why, and how to incorporate your values and beliefs into your parenting. You are also likely to reflect on your own childhood. You might think about how your parents or guardians parented and whether that worked or didn't work for you.

For some people, thinking about how they were raised might give them ideas for what approaches they want to copy from their own childhood. Perhaps you were spanked, and you decide not to do that. Perhaps you had a parent who spent a lot of time reading to you, and you want to replicate that behavior. Reflecting in this way can be an interesting and beneficial activity.

For some of us, especially those who might have had queer-phobic experiences in childhood, becoming a parent may involve realizing that perhaps we were hurt or failed by those who were supposed to take care of us. That can be painful or infuriating to recognize. It might make you change how you relate to your parents —you might cut them out of your life, for instance, or you might place different boundaries around your relationship, or you might decide your parents aren't safe or trustworthy enough to babysit your kids. It might bring up memories or thoughts you'd repressed. You might find your emotions vacillating all over the place.

As I said before, in the section on trauma, all your experiences here are valid. You might feel grateful to your parents for all they've done for you, or you might feel furious that they didn't know how to best support you, or you might feel any other of a large range of emotions. Be kind to yourself as you go through this process and do what you need to in order to move forward, whether that's chatting with a friend, journaling, therapy, art classes, or whatever else. Needless to say, try not to repeat the worst of the behaviors you've seen or to take any of your pain out on your children.

For many people, parenting is one of the most important and meaningful activities they'll ever do, especially if they have consciously and willingly chosen to embark on being a parent, the way most LGBTQ+ folks have. Take your time to consider your childhood and to connect it to who you are today and how you want to be as a parent. Allow your thoughts on this subject to progress and change over the years. No one is perfect and most of us have parents who did what they could, even if it wasn't always the right thing for us. Remember that our children, too, will probably have their complaints about our parenting. Being conscious and conscientious about how you've become who you are, what you're doing, and why you're doing it will stand you in good stead as a parent.

Parental Leave

Earlier, we talked about giving yourself some time to recover from the process of adding to your family. For many people, this may include taking a few weeks or months off work. In some countries, this is a given and all new parents get paid time off, while in other places, people have to use their vacation days or take unpaid leave. This is clearly unfair, as everyone could do with paid time off to focus on their family. I mean, from the cold perspective of the bottom line, employers would get more out of their employees if they treated them well and offered a good range of benefits. Relaxed, grateful employees might work harder and more efficiently, and thereby earn more money for their employers but from the larger human perspective, giving people generous amounts of time to spend with their new family members is simply the right thing to do. We're not machines, able to work nonstop, and we can't be loving, patient, and attentive parents if we're struggling to balance our jobs and our homelife, and if we're desperately working all the hours we can in order to pay our bills.

In the UK, parents are entitled to parental leave or adoption leave. There are different rules around this, depending on how long you have worked for a company or institution and on whether your employer simply follows UK law or whether they add on extra benefits. Traditionally, the birth parent, if there is one, has been given the most amount of leave, which, in many ways, makes sense, given the need to have a recovery period from the physical work of pregnancy and birth and to establish breastfeeding or chestfeeding. However, it doesn't have to be this way, if that doesn't work well for your family. You could split the leave evenly, or you could both be off at the same time, or you could arrange something altogether different. In the UK, surrogates also get parental leave, even though they generally are not with the baby, because they, too, need time to recover.

In the U.S., the system is much more piecemeal, as the U.S. is the least generous Western country when it comes to leave (Arneson, 2021). Indeed, the U.S. is the wealthiest country in the world to not have a nationalized system of paid parental leave at all. Parents can take a certain number of weeks of unpaid leave (currently 12 weeks), but this is obviously problematic, because not everyone can afford 3 months without an income. Also, 3 months is not enough time for most people to get to know their new family member. As in the UK, some organizations and companies in the U.S. choose to offer additional time off, with or without pay, which means that two families living next door to each other who each bring a new child into their home at the same time might have drastically different experiences of parental leave.

Another challenge is that not all employers and countries recognize LGBTQ+ relationships, so if one partner in a relationship is the one who gave birth or is on the adoption or birth certificate, the employer might not feel that the other partner (or partners) is entitled to parental leave. This is clearly unfair, and if you come across this, you may need to involve your HR department, union, and/or lawyer.

In many places, including the U.S., there are movements aimed at improving and equalizing the parental leave system. For now, you will want to talk to your employer while you are in the process of adding to your family in order to find out what you are entitled to, and perhaps to argue your case for additional benefits or a more flexible approach. You might discover, for instance, that your employer will allow you to return to work part-time instead of full-time or to do hybrid working, so you can work from home some days. You might even pave the way for the next generation of LGBTQ+ parents to have more options for parental leave.

A Stor. About Parental Leave

Amy, a gender non-conforming butch lesbian who works at a university, shared parental leave with her partner, a bisexual cis woman. She writes:

"We moved from Scotland to England while my partner was pregnant with our son. She had taken a new job and so was only entitled to statutory maternity leave. We also thought it would be good for me to be able to have a large chunk of time off with the baby so we could have some bonding time. We thought this was something worth prioritizing for me, as the non-biological parent.

In the end, she had 10 weeks off (three of which were annual leave) and I had 7 months of parental leave. It was quite a faff to sort it all out.

The university where I worked at the time was great. I had plenty of support from HR and they never questioned my use of shared parental leave. They had no previous experience of anyone else doing anything similar, so they had to work it all out from scratch. They'd had people sharing leave with a partner but in those cases, the university employee was the birth mother.

The head of HR for the school I was working in ended up consulting with others on a dedicated online forum for HR leads in higher education to see if anyone had facilitated shared parental leave and could share templates, agreements, etc. I hope others have made use of it since!"

Paperwork

Sorry, sorry. No one likes paperwork. Well, okay, I'm sure some people like paperwork, but most of us find it tiring and irritating. The frustration and annoyance increase when you're dealing with heteronormative paperwork.

Let's face it, most things connected with family-formation are centered around heterosexual and cisgender people. That can be quite upsetting, especially if you're already feeling vulnerable (having a child is surely one of the most stressful times in your life, even if you wanted a child and are thrilled to have them).

Depending on where you live, you may find that most forms you need to fill in only allow for a "mother" and a "father." Sure, that may describe your situation well, but it also might not be accurate at all. Understandably, you may not wish to use those terms, so you may well balk at signing those forms.

What can you do? Well, one couple complained. This couple, Gemma and Kate Fox, went to the British Broadcasting Corporation (BBC) and because of the publicity, eventually the people responsible for the various documents, forms, and websites at their doctor's office, their local council, and elsewhere agreed to make changes (Carr, 2021). They were told to just cross out the incorrect terms on the forms, which, frankly, isn't good enough, although it's certainly an option, if that's what you want to do (I've done that at times).

Why can't the forms be more inclusive? It's not hard to just write "parent" instead of gendered terms. This couple, Gemma and Kate Fox, went to the British Broadcasting Corporation (BBC) and because of the publicity, eventually the people responsible for the various documents, forms, and websites at their doctor's office, their local council, and elsewhere agreed to make changes (Carr 2021). As the Foxes said, however, the forms were also limited regarding ethnicity and religion, so clearly governmental authorities, health professionals, and agencies need to do better in general.

Another paperwork issue is how some places require you to prove your relationship to your partner and/or child. Some people have mentioned being asked extremely intrusive questions (such as about their sex lives) when they're applying to adopt or trying to get fertility treatment. Others have said they have to gather years' worth of evidence to attest how long they've been with their partner or spouse, or to demonstrate that they've been present in the life of a child that they didn't physically give birth to. It must be dreadful to be busy parenting and getting to know your little one while also being asked to validate who and what you are to that child.

If you feel erased or bothered by the paperwork you have to deal with, or if you otherwise have not been treated fairly and without prejudice, you have a number of choices, none of them ideal because they all push the emotional and practical labor on to you. You can just get on with filling in the forms as they are, or you can fill them in but cross out the inaccurate/inapplicable words or sections. You can complain to the relevant company, organization, agency, etc. about their forms. You might also want to get in touch with journalists, as the Foxes did with the BBC, with lawyers, or with an LGBTQ+ rights organization (as one of the couples mentioned doing above; they complained to Stonewall about how they were treated by their fertility clinic).

Queer history shows that changes are only made when we fight for our rights and when we speak up. Being an activist while you have a new baby or child in the house isn't necessarily what you want to do (though it might be), but if you have the mental, emotional, and physical energy, please do complain vocally. Governmental agencies or doctor's offices won't know what they need to do to change unless we tell them. So, where possible, let's use our voices and encourage people to make paperwork more inclusive.

Names

One of the questions I receive most often is what my wife and I are called by our children. I am not totally sure why this is of such interest to people, but I guess some can't think beyond the one-mom, one-dad family norm, while others seem to feel that hearing our titles will somehow tell them which one of us is the "real" mother (spoiler alert: we're both the real mothers). Frankly, I'd be a bit better off these days if I got money each time someone asked, "So is one of you called Dad?" I always say, "Well, no, because there isn't a dad."

Sometimes it's worth reminding ourselves—and those asking us these questions—that even in relationships with two presumably opposite-sex parents, there is flexibility around names. Not all female parents relate to words such as mom, mommy, mum, mummy, momma, mama, ma, or mother. Similarly, not all male parents like dad, daddy, pa, papa, pop, pops, or father. Let's not get started on names for grandparents, aunts, uncles, or other relatives. Some people prefer to use a name in another language or want to be called by their first name or a nickname. In some families, children decide what their parents are called. There could be a combination of things happening, with parents using one term when their children are little, and then a different term later, and still another term at a further point in time.

So, what should your children call you? If your baby or child is little, it's up to you, and even if they're older, you can have some input. Think about what terms you feel comfortable with and if they best reflect the way you think of your gender and your role in your child's life. Be creative, if that's what's right for you. I'm hearing more and more people play around with language to come up with new, often gender-non-specific terms, such as mapa, baba, poppy, moddy, par or pare, zaza, and more. Don't feel you have to stick with traditional terms.

If you do get those silly questions, it's up to you whether to answer people, challenge their assumptions, or change the subject. Meanwhile, see Appendix 5 for some suggested answers to nosy comments.

What to Tell People?

The last section began to get into the topic of how we answer all those questions that we get as non-heterosexual and/or non-cisgender and/or otherwise non-majority families. It's not easy to know how to respond, because often we do want to be polite or to help educate those who don't know so much about it, but at the same time, we are individuals, and we have a right to privacy. We don't have to tell every single person we meet everything about ourselves.

Oh, how we get ourselves tied in knots when we worry about what we're going to say to people about our identity! Some of us have been through that dance, avoiding using pronouns when we talk about our partners, or trying not to be engaged in personal discussions in the workplace, or not telling the truth when we're in places of worship, or otherwise feeling worried about whether we're going to be accepted for who we are. This gets even more complicated when we think about explaining how we produced our children.

In *Let's Talk About Hard Things*, a book filled with suggestions and stories about how to discuss challenging topics, Anna Sale (2021) suggests raising topics by saying, "I've been wondering about something" or "I need to tell you something I haven't" (p. 11). Common advice about telling people something personal notes that you could also add in a sentence or two about how you're feeling about what you are going to say and what you're worried the other person might say or do in response and what you'd like to happen. All this might work well if you need to come out about your sexuality or gender identity (among other topics). For example, you might say, "I have something to talk to you about. I feel quite nervous, because I don't know if you'll still like me and accept me. But I hope we can talk about this honestly and openly, and still be friends." But what do you do when it's other people who are trying to force you to answer their (sometimes prurient) questions? This can feel somehow even more personal and challenging. How do you reply?

When it comes to curious adults, I base my decision about what to say on a few factors. One is how I feel on a given day and whether I want to spend time educating people about LGBTQ+ families. I'm a teacher and I love teaching, but I need time off too and sometimes I'm just not in the mood for being the token queer. Another point is to try to figure out why those people are asking. If they are simply being nosy, I don't usually share, but if they are asking out of a real desire to learn, then I might give them some general information or point to other resources, such as websites or, well, this book. I also think about the context, that is, the where and the how of the conversation. If they are asking me in a bold or rude manner in front of lots of other people, I'm more likely to respond with general facts and some humor, whereas if it's an intimate one-to-one conversation, I might be more inclined to chat. Once when someone asked me in a restaurant, as we were eating breakfast, "So, where and how did you get the sperm and what did you do with it?" I felt the only polite response was, "I don't think that's a good conversation to have while we're enjoying a meal."

Often, people seem to think that because you belong to a particular group, you're always going to be willing to represent that group and to talk about issues related to that group. Sometimes that's absolutely fine but, as you know, at other points we just want to relax and be left alone. Sometimes we want to be treated and respected as full humans, in all our complexity, and not merely as a member of a specific identity or affinity group. It's okay to tell people that now is not the time for this conversation or that you're not able or willing to share that information. It might be more useful to direct them to other sources, as a way of reminding them to do their own research ("Let me Google that for you").

In regard to what to tell your own children, my advice would always be the truth. If you normalize your family and regularly discuss how the children were conceived or how they joined you, it won't seem shocking or upsetting for them. It might even just be a boring story that their parents drone on about. Whereas if you try to hide facts or if you express shame or embarrassment, your children will pick up on it and perhaps get angry or upset with you. There are a lot of children's picture books these days that show different family arrangements and some of them even explain how the babies were made. If you're not sure what to say, you can use one of these books to start with. My own favorite is *What Makes a Baby* by Cory Silverberg, with illustrations by Fiona Smyth (2013), because it is gender-neutral and ethnicity-neutral, and it includes questions and space so you can add information that is relevant to your own story.[9] You could also read a book or watch a film with two mothers or two fathers or whatever else might be relevant to you and then use that as a stepping-stone for a deeper conversation by saying, "Doesn't that family seem a bit like ours?" or "What do you think about that family?" or something similar.

Be open and honest and answer their questions. Even if you don't think you have the right words, try. My view is that there is always an age-appropriate way to talk to children about conception and identity—and indeed, every other topic—so get to know your child and find a path that works well for you both. They'll appreciate your efforts. With time, they'll know they can come to you for an honest conversation on any topic; that is a great basis for a strong relationship.

Advice on Being Honest with Children

H is a queer/bisexual polyamorous woman who produced and raises her son in a poly, coparenting relationship. She writes:

"I would recommend living as openly as possible. My family have been privileged to have been honest about our situation throughout. In doing so, I hope we have helped some other people to live more honestly along the way. People are often more positive than unpleasant when they hear about the details and have their questions answered calmly.

The main worry I've heard is, 'Isn't your child confused?' The

---

9 By the way, I wrote a book about LGBTQ+ books for children and young adults, *Are the Kids All Right?* (Epstein, 2013). If you're interested in finding some reading material that features people like you and families like yours that you can read to or with your kids, you could check out my book, which includes a reading list. If you read languages other than English, my more recent book, *International LGBTQ+ Literature for Children and Young Adults*, may interest you too (Epstein & Chapman, 2021).

answer is, of course not. Children are confused when people lie to them or keep things from them, which we have never done. We have never let people continue in the assumption that S and I are together, or that F was conceived within a romantic relationship. F totally understands and accepts his family structure because all of his questions are answered honestly."

Of course, it's a slightly different matter if your children have grown up with you presenting in one way regarding your gender and sexuality, and then you want to tell them that things have changed or that they were different from what you previously said (Sale, 2021). I mean, you might be excited about how your life has progressed and you may be ready to have this conversation. You might have practiced in your head exactly what you're going to say, and your children could be receptive and understanding. You might also be feeling awkward or unsure about things yourself, you might not know how much detail to go into, you might be facing pressure from your spouse or other relatives or friends not to tell the kids, or your children might suspect something is going on and try to avoid talking to you. For understandable reasons, you could be putting off the talk.

Still, you probably will want to push through the discomfort, because these conversations are worth having. Just as you want to show your children that you love and accept them for who they are, you want to give them the chance to know, accept, and love the real you. You don't necessarily need to give them intimate details about your sex life—although if that's the sort of open relationship you have in your family, that might be appropriate—and you don't need to describe your entire journey in great depth. Perhaps you don't fully understand it all yourself, or they might not be ready or willing to hear it. However, you can approach the subject honestly and with an open heart, and ask them to do the same. Also, think about how you frame things. If you tell them that you're happy to better know yourself now, that sets them up to also be happy for you, whereas if you express shame, anger, or anxiety, they will pick up on that and begin to feel that way too.

While you can't control the reactions from your children (or anyone else), you can control what you say and what impression you attempt to give, and how you handle the discussion. Allow your kids to ask and say whatever they need to without you getting offended. Recognize that this is likely news to your children and that they are entitled to their feelings and opinions, including shock, disappointment, fear, and pain. You can and should expect politeness; there's no need for name-calling or slurs. If your children can't have this conversation without being rude, you have the right to suggest that you stop talking about it now and come back to the subject when everyone's feeling calmer.

With time and plenty of openness, your children will, I hope, absorb your news and be ready to move forward with you. Naturally, they will continue to have their feelings about it all, and these emotions may change from day to day. Also, your news may affect their lives in more dramatic ways, such as if you are making plans for a separation, surgery, new ways of you presenting yourself, a move to a new location, and so on. While it's tempting to focus on yourself and your exciting new discovery of who you really are, continue to be a sensitive partner and parent, recognizing that this might be tough on your spouse and children in ways they don't always feel able to express to you. Think through what might make the most practical sense for your family. For instance, maybe your new partner won't move in right away or at all, or maybe you'll allow your kids to call you what they usually did instead of your new preferred term, or maybe the children will stay in the house while the parents take turns living in a different apartment.

You and your children have a vested interest in being a strong family unit. Being honest with each other and showing one another love, trust, and respect is key to having good relationships.

A Stor, About Coming Out to Children Later In Life 🖉

Olga, a queer woman, had children while married to a man. She later met a woman and fell in love. Here, she describes how she came out to her children:

"'What would you do if one of your children turns out to be homosexual?' The question was asked in a sewing group in the 1970s, where my mother participated. I can imagine that it was a charged question at the time, especially in a small place like where I grew up. My mom just said, "Then I would love them even more, because I think they would need that to face the world."

My mom and dad did not have to love me more than they already did, because when I met my girlfriend, attitudes, at least where we live, had changed. I think that it might be a challenge for some to come out as queer. However, for me, as a person, it was not a big thing. It is love, that is all. Nevertheless, being a mom of three preteen boys, living in a small town, and coming out was somewhat worrisome for me at first.

I guess my thoughts went like my mom's; I was afraid that it would be difficult for my children and that they would have to suffer from my choice to live in a non-normative relationship. So, I prepared myself. I read a lot and I talked with the school welfare officers, family therapists, and other people in the same situation. Although, when I finally told my children, it turned out that the big thing for them was not that I had met another woman, but rather, that I had met someone at all. In the beginning, it was not easy for them to accept that someone else shared my love and attention, and that it was no longer just the four of us. With time, I think that everyone's relationships have developed and that our family life is much smoother today.

Furthermore, my girlfriend and I have decided not to live together for now. This is a conscious decision, not only for the children's sake, but also for us adults. It is for us a way to avoid tensions and stress, as well as to give everyone the time and space needed. As a mother and a girlfriend, I try to share my time the best I can between the four of them. Sometimes my girlfriend and I would like to spend more time together, but we try to focus on what is best for everyone right now, and to see it from a larger perspective. One day, my children will not live at home any longer, and then my girlfriend and I will move in together. I think it would have been different if we had met when my kids were younger, but instead, we met when they were right in a precarious period in life in many ways, so for all of us, this was the best solution.

For my family, I think it has been extremely important that we have talked a lot during this first period, to be as sensitive to everyone's needs as possible. We have been clear about the fact that she is not another mom for my children; she is an important additional adult in our family, and she is my girlfriend. I am pleased that she can provide other perspectives and ideas, but also practical help for them that I cannot. Most of all, I am sincerely grateful that our relationship can show my children a good example of how it can be to live in a relationship filled with tenderness, warmth, and love. I am more than thankful to be able to transfer this to my children."

It gets a bit trickier with other people's kids, however. If your children's friends ask questions, I suggest answering them as honestly as you feel able, without getting into details that their parents might not be ready for them to hear (even if the kids themselves are ready to hear them). Being factual and calm tends to work for children, so you could say, for example, "No, [child's name] doesn't have a mommy, because we're a two-dad family." or "Well, [child's name] was adopted, which means they grew in someone else's tummy and then came to live with us. We're so glad they joined our family." It's often a good idea to tell the parents of these children about the conversations you've been having, so they are prepared for further questions. If those parents get angry that you've had a supposedly inappropriate conversation, then be proud you've done the child a service by being honest with them when their parents aren't necessarily able to be. Most relatively liberal and understanding parents will be grateful that you've been willing to talk, because they might not have known how. And unless you were suddenly talking about, you know, S-E-X, the topic many parents seem to dread, you won't have done anything that anyone can really complain about.

See Appendix 5 for some suggested responses to nosy or curious questions. I'm sure you'll be able to add even more ideas to that list. You could always get in touch and tell me what they are.

Bear in mind that no matter what you say or how kind and polite and open you are, there will be people who won't like it. To be honest, if people can't cope with what you want or need to tell them, it's up to you to decide whether these are people who should be in your life. Maybe they need time to adjust or maybe they never will. You know them best, and you also know what works for you and your family. You need to feel safe, comfortable, and accepted, so you have to decide who to have in your life and how much information to give them. It could be that you need to cut off contact, perhaps temporarily, or it could be that you will reach a point of deepened understanding and affection. Accept yourself, be true to who you are, and answer questions to the best of your ability, if you want to. It's up to other people to handle it or not.

Feeding

Nourishing Your Baby

Let's say you've got a baby. You know you need to keep that baby alive and that infants can only have milk. How on earth are you going to feed the baby? What are your options and how do they relate to you being LGBTQ+? Amazingly, we queer parents have even more possible ways of feeding our young than non-LGBTQ+ folks. Aren't we lucky?

Breastfeeding/Nursing/Lactating

Humans are mammals, and mammals are defined as a group in part because we feed our babies from our mammary glands. Breastfeeding (also called nursing, lactating, or chestfeeding but see below for more on this term) is the biological norm. It's how humans, and other mammals, have survived across all these generations.

Breastmilk helps a baby grow and develop optimally. Also, the act of breastfeeding brings the breastfeeding parent and the breastfed child (or children) closer. It can prevent illness in both the child and the parent. Human milk is tailor-made for human babies, so rather than discussing the so-called benefits of it, it is better to refer to the risks involved in feeding formula milk. In other words, human milk is what human babies need to have, whenever possible

We don't often see breastfeeding in public or in the media, such as in films or on TV or in literature[10], whereas bottle-feeding is prevalent In our society today, so sometimes, it can seem uncommon or even unnatural. It is, of course, what we have evolved do, even if we now mostly consider breasts to be sexual (Young, 2016, p. 145).

There is no single right way to breastfeed. There are multiple positions, such as cradle, cross-cradle, rugby/football, koala,

---

10 In my most recent book, *The Portrayals of Breastfeeding in Literature*, I analyze how breastfeeding is depicted in books for adults and children (Woodstein, 2021). It may not surprise you to hear that breastfeeding is often portrayed as negative or problematic in English-language literature; this is not true of literature in all other languages, however, which shows how much societal perceptions influence cultural or media depictions, and vice versa.

laid-back, and side-lying, and some might work better than others for a particular parent-child combination, so you need to find what suits you best. You might also prefer to feed on a sofa, in bed, or in a sling or in the bath. Some people prefer to feed while covered up or while on your own with your baby rather than in public, although you certainly don't have to. In other words, you and your baby will want to experiment until you figure out how you feed best. Look on Google or YouTube to see some of these positions.

Other useful things to know are that humans can breastfeed two or more children at the same time (often called tandem-feeding). So, you can keep feeding an older child while pregnant, if you want to, and when the little one is born, or you can feed two children, whether of different ages or twins (or triplets or more). Natural-term weaning—in other words, breastfeeding until a child and parent mutually choose to stop—usually happens between the ages of two and seven years old. Biologist Katie Hinde's research suggests a weaning age of between eighteen months and ten years old, depending on various factors (2016) and anthropologist Kathy Dettwyler suggests between 3 and 4 years old, although she notes that it can go up to seven (1997). The World Health Organization recommends that people breastfeed at least until the age of 2, for optimum health (physical and mental) for you and the baby.

Many people enjoy breastfeeding in part because our society treats breasts as solely sexual objects, only there for the pleasure of men. So, it can be satisfying and also activist to use them for another purpose, one that is sometimes looked down upon these days. It can also be satisfying to know that your body is nourishing your child and that you are building a connection with your baby in this way.

One of the most important things to know about breastfeeding is that if you are finding it challenging in any way, you should get support as soon as you can, whether from your midwife, doctor, doula, lactation consultant, local support group, or a friend or relative. Nearly all breastfeeding issues can be fixed with some help, and, it is, in fact, relatively uncommon for someone not to be able to breastfeed if they want to[11], so try to call a breastfeeding helpline or get to a group or see a professional. You don't have to accept people brushing you off, diminishing your concerns, or encouraging you to just swap to formula. It's known that people who want to breastfeed but end up not doing so, or not doing so for as long as they want, feel grief about it that can last the rest of their lives (Brown, 2019).

It may be useful for you to know that breastfeeding/nursing is something that happens throughout the day and night.

> Many breastfed babies feed 12 times or even more in 24 hours, and this can be at seemingly random times of the day rather than every two hours on the dot. Sometimes they feed several times in quick succession; other times they'll have a longer break. This is absolutely normal (Brown, 2021, pp. 58-59).

As Amy Brown points out, we grown-ups don't always follow a set pattern in terms of when we eat and how much we eat. We might have three big meals one day, but snacks and then just one larger meal another day, or we might not be especially hungry on yet another day. It makes sense that babies, too, vary how much they feed throughout the day and from day to day. They might have a pattern for a while and then this could change, perhaps due to a growth spurt, teething, a developmental leap, a vacation across time zones, an exciting activity, or for no apparent reason at all. It's

---

11 You might struggle to breastfeed/chestfeed if you have hypoplastic breasts, if you have had certain kinds of breast/chest surgery, or in a few other situations. Sometimes, getting help will make a difference. For example, if you have polycystic ovary syndrome or diabetes, and want to breastfeed/chestfeed, seek out professional support. There are also some relatively rare cases where breastfeeding/chestfeeding probably isn't the right choice. For example, you might not be able to nurse your baby if you are undergoing radiation therapy, if you have HIV (although this depends on where you live and some other circumstances, such as if you are taking antiretroviral therapy), or if you are taking certain medications that are not safe for the baby. In some situations, there may be alternative, breastfeeding-compatible medications you can take, so again, speak to an expert. If you want to breastfeed/chestfeed but cannot, you may have some big feelings about that, so be sure you talk to your partner, friends, therapist, or anyone else you feel comfortable with, so you aren't left alone, feeling sad.

generally considered best for establishing breastfeeding to feed on demand, as and when the baby wants it. You can also offer the breast because you want to; breastfeeding is comforting and healthy for both you and the baby.

Pros and Cons of Breastfeeding/Nursing

PROS	CONS
Human milk is individualized for each child and provides protection from illness in both the short- and long-term.	Your family or friends who did not breastfeed may challenge your choice to do so.
Breastmilk is free (though the labor involved in breastfeeding should be valued).	You may get comments for breastfeeding in public or in front of others.
Most people can do it.	You may get pressured to share the feeding of the baby.
Breastfeeding is about more than nutrition; it provides comfort and a bond.	
If you want to, you can still express some milk so your partner can feed the baby.	
Both you and your baby get a major oxytocin boost when feeding.	
Breastfeeding goes against the current societal idea that breasts are just for men's pleasure or to sell objects.	

A Stor, About Breastfeeding

Earlier in this book, Perse and Deb, a lesbian couple, told us about how they became a blended family, how they extended their family, and how Deb birthed their younger two children at home.

Here, Deb writes about her choice to breastfeed:

"My decision to breastfeed was based on my desire to experience breastfeeding as an integral part of attachment parenting (we also co-sleep with our baby and toddler), and to ensure that I was able to share antibodies with my babies while their immune systems were immature. I was also inspired by my wife's experience of extended breastfeeding; she fed her first child until she was 2 and a half years old, simultaneously alongside her second child for a year of that time, and fed her younger one until he was 2 years old.

I breastfed our son until he self-weaned at 18 months, by which time, I was 3 months pregnant with our second child. I am currently breastfeeding our daughter, with the intention of continuing to feed her until she also self-weans. I have had the great privilege of being able to take a year-long maternity break for each of my two children, which has been invaluable to continuity of breastfeeding on demand."

Another Stor, About Breastfeeding

Blanche and Esme, a lesbian couple originally from France, each gestated and breastfed one of their children. They explain why:

"Once our son was born, we decided to breastfeed, as it seemed obvious that it was better for his health. It is true that with formula you know exactly how much the baby is feeding and vitamin deficiencies are extremely rare, but I had a healthy, balanced diet and I was confident the baby was having enough milk so there didn't seem to be any downside to breastfeeding. On top of the immunity, I could pass to him, we were interested in the fact that there is some evidence that breastfeeding is protective for asthma, and there are a few asthmatics in my family, so we thought it was worth a try."

Chestfeeding/Bodyfeeding

I'll say this at the outset; some people worry that by using terms such as chestfeeding or bodyfeeding, we're erasing words such as breastfeeding or nursing, and invalidating their meaning. I disagree with this. By adding additional terms, ones that make people feel comfortable, we're making things more inclusive. If you want to describe what you do as breastfeeding, then you should use that term. If someone else wants to say chestfeeding—even if you think they seem like the same thing—then that's their choice. It doesn't have to affect the words you use for yourself or how you feel about what you do. Adding more words doesn't mean taking away the words or concepts that you prefer for yourself.

Okay, now that I've got that off my chest (so to speak), let's discuss chestfeeding and bodyfeeding.[12] Like breastfeeding, it means feeding your baby at your chest with your own milk and it is optimal for the baby, and for you.

However, if you identify as nonbinary or trans, you may experience some additional gender dysphoria if your mammary tissue grows during pregnancy or during the course of feeding, and you may feel uncomfortable with feeding itself. In our society, feeding a baby from your body is often seen as something females do, and if you do not identify as female, it can be challenging to be perceived

---

12 Interestingly, in an article on transmasculine people and chestfeeding, one person uses the phrase "mammal feeding" (MacDonald et al., 2016, n.p.). I've never seen that anywhere else, so I won't use it here, but it's good to think of it as an option for terminology.

as doing a supposedly female-only thing, such as lactating. In one research study on transmasculine individuals, the authors note advice suggesting that trans men try to "asexualize" their breasts, but as they point out, "it is unclear how this strategy might be implemented." (MacDonald et al., 2016, n.p.). Keep in mind, though, that you don't have to listen to societal stereotypes and that chest-feeding is about you and your baby, not about what other people think. You can absolutely be male, masculine, or nonbinary and feed your baby directly from your body. However you feel about your chest area is acceptable.

If you do find that the dysphoria is too tough for you and you need to stop feeding, you want to get surgery, or you're ready to return to hormones or begin taking hormones for the first time, remember that it is your body and your choice. There is help to get, if you want to talk through your options with someone. You could, for instance, choose to express milk instead of feeding directly at your chest, or you could decide to only feed at certain times or in particular places, or you could use donated human milk.

One thing to be aware of if you are chestfeeding is that if you have had chest masculinization surgery (sometimes called top surgery) or are taking certain hormones or drugs, you may struggle to fully feed your baby yourself. This is because of how much mammary tissue has been removed or how the hormones are affecting your body. In that case, you may still be able to provide some of the human milk your baby needs, and you can top that up with donor milk or formula milk. If you like, you can use a supplemental nursing system, feeding the child the additional milk while they are still latched on to you. You may want or need to be extra careful of your chest area, depending on how recently you had your chest masculinization surgery.

If you haven't yet had chest masculinization surgery but are considering it or are on a waiting list to get it, you could consider holding off until after you are done reproducing and feeding. This may not feel possible for you, however. If you do go for it before having a baby, talk to your surgeon about what techniques they are using and what this might mean for you in terms of feeding your baby.

Whether you have had surgery or not, and whether you are feeding your baby from your body or not, you may still experience some of the issues other feeders do, such as engorgement or mastitis. Given how little research there is on trans and nonbinary chestfeeders (de la Cretaz, 2016), some healthcare providers may be surprised or may not know how to best support you through this. So, be prepared to do research and to tell your doctor, midwife, IBCLC, or whoever else what you think is going on and what you need. It isn't fair that this burden should be placed on you, and hopefully it won't be, but educating yourself around what will happen to your body during pregnancy and the postpartum period will be beneficial in many ways.

Depending on your situation, you may want to get professional support with chestfeeding/bodyfeeding, so you will want to seek out an LGBTQ+-friendly and knowledgeable IBCLC.

Pros and Cons of Chestfeeding/Bodyfeeding

PROS	CONS
Human milk is individualized for each child and provides protection from illness in both the short- and long-term	You may find it dysphoric to feed or to see changes to your body.
You are providing comfort and nutrition to your child.	You might find it uncomfortable to feed in public, depending on your relationship with your body.
Your milk is free and always available.	You may struggle to feed, depending on whether you have had surgery and/or are taking hormones.

You can continue to feed your baby at your chest while also using donor milk or formula milk.	
You may find that using your body to feed your baby provides you with a new sense of appreciation for the body you were born with.	

A Note on Binding

If you bind your chest, you may want to continue doing so through pregnancy and lactation, especially if it is important to your mental and emotional health.

However, you will also want to listen to the physical signals from your body. If your chest feels tender, delicate, sore, or otherwise different during pregnancy or lactation, you may choose not to bind, to bind less tightly, to bind for short amounts of time, to bind only in some situations and not others, or to generally be flexible around binding.

It is usually thought to be better not to compress the mammary tissue during lactation, especially when establishing the milk supply. For this reason, people are also encouraged to wear soft bras or undershirts, not those with underwire. So, you may prefer not to bind during the first couple of months, depending on your situation.

It is important to know that binding may impact your milk supply, so you may want to consider your goals for feeding.

If you do bind, you might want to gradually increase the amount of time you spend with a binder on, so your body gets used to it.

If you feel you need support with lactation, including with decisions around binding, it may be worth seeing a lactation consultant.

Chestfeeding your child may bring up a range of feelings, such as increased dysphoria, pride, confusion, worry, happiness, and more. Breastfeeding/chestfeeding groups, counselors, and lactation consultants can help you through this.

A Stor, About Chestfeeding[13]

Codi defines himself as transgender and chestfed his child. He didn't intend to do so, however. Codi writes:

"When my daughter was born, I wasn't going to chestfeed her because of the dysphoria around that part of my body.

But she wouldn't take her bottles, so I stuck it out, so I'd know she was having some milk.

The feeling I had when I chestfed my little girl was a weird one, to say the least. I didn't want to do it but then I also loved the bond it created."

13 There are some additional chestfeeding stories in a research article on trans men and infant feeding. For example, "One of the most supportive communities I found during my pregnancy was the La Leche League community, which my midwife was heavily involved in. And she got me connected to a lot of other people and they were just so accepting and warm and gracious...I also really wanted that relationship with my child. I wanted that connection, you know, of holding my child, my own child, to my chest, being connected in that way and being able to offer that not just nourishing but nurturing aspect" (MacDonald et al., 2016, n.p.). A slightly different perspective is from a different transmasculine individual: "even with the nursing I don't think I'm going to do extended. Like, I might last a couple months but you know I'm going to want to be back on testosterone and because I present as female during the pregnancy, and I can only live my life as being seen as female for so long" (MacDonald et al., 2016, n.p.). There are other transmasculine stories and more information in that article, which I recommend you read.

Another Stor, About Chestfeeding

Kaedan, a genderqueer/non-binary person who birthed and nursed both their children, is partnered with a cis man. Kaedan writes the following about chestfeeding:

"With regards to breast/chestfeeding, I nursed my children from birth. I love nursing and feel grateful that it went fairly smoothly for my kids and me.

I personally didn't feel any dysphoria or identity discomfort in the process of nursing. However, I am looking forward to when I could use a binder again. I used one sometimes before I was pregnant with my first child, and then nursed my first pretty much up until I got pregnant with second, so I haven't used a binder in 4-5 years. It will be nice to have the option of doing that again after I'm done nursing my youngest.

For me, the hardest part about nursing (and pregnancy/being a parent in general) is the way my gender identity was made invisible. I already look female and get misgendered often, so add into that pregnancy/nursing and it's so automatic in people's minds to assume they are talking to a cisgender woman.

It felt especially alienating in so-called 'mom's groups' with my first child. Because of how family/parental leave works in the U.S., it's more typical that only the gestational parent will get extended time off, so the people who were attending the 'baby-and-me' events were typically the gestational parents, who overwhelmingly were cis women. They assumed I was as well, and often, I wasn't in the headspace or didn't feel comfortable enough to correct them, so it kind of felt like I was 'playing a part' while at those events.

There was a lot of compartmentalization going on in my

mind. It was easier the second time around, partly because I more carefully chose who I spent time with during my parental leave, and also because COVID forced a lot of those groups to shut down, so there just wasn't the same level of opportunity to get misgendered if you are mostly home all the time."

Co-Feeding

Co-feeding means there are two or more parents who are lactating and who can feed the child or children. It could be that both parents have gestated and given birth, either around the same time, or with some months or even years apart. Perhaps one has given birth and the other has re-lactated or induced lactation (more on this below). Maybe one is lactating and the other uses a supplemental nursing system (SNS).[14] Whatever the exact circumstances, there are two or more people who are able to feed the little one or ones. Throughout history, people have fed each other's babies, so this is nothing new. There have been wet nurses, of course, but there have also been practical benefits to, for example, someone temporarily handing off their baby to a sibling or cousin or friend who also had milk.

Some cultures even have the term "milk siblings" to denote two people who aren't biological siblings but have shared milk from the same source. Due to this belief that sharing milk creates "milk kinship," and the later potential impact on people not being able to marry those they are "milk siblings" with, some people might have strong ideas about who they are willing to co-feed with. This concept has been particularly researched in Islamic culture (Subudhi & Sriraman, 2021), but it exists elsewhere too.

There are some immediately obvious advantages to co-feeding. The baby gets to bond with two or more adults, gaining nutrition and nurturing from multiple sources. The parents can each get a

---

14 A supplemental nursing system (SNS) is a tube that you attach to your breast/chest and that leads to a pouch/container that you fill with milk. Your child feeds at the breast/chest and may get some milk directly from you but also gets milk through the SNS.

break at times and if one parent has to go to work or is otherwise occupied, the baby or child still gets fed. It can also be a lovely experience for two or more adults to share feeding in this way.

The parents may have to work out whether they will feel jealous if the other parent feeds the baby they themselves gestated and birthed or if they might be upset if one parent seems to be the preferred one (then again, children often go through a stage of preferring one parent over another). The adults might also need to consider who will feed and when, depending on their schedules. They could ponder in advance how they will feel if one of them ends up not being able or willing to co-feed, despite their plans. It may be, for instance, that one parent has a more copious milk supply, perhaps due to feeding the child more often.

While co-feeding may not often be seen or discussed in Western society today, it certainly isn't unusual in terms of human behavior, and it can be a beneficial and practically useful way of feeding babies.

Pros and Cons of Co-Feeding

PROS	CONS
The baby/child gets food and bonding with two or more parents.	If one parent doesn't feed as often, they might have a lower milk supply and/or feel less involved.
Parents can work, have a break, or do other things without worrying about their child being fed.	There may be some jealousy or other difficult emotions around feeding.
Two or more parents can feel intimately involved in childcare.	

Advice on Co-Feeding

Zoe Faulkner, a heterosexual, cisgender IBCLC, has worked with many LGBTQ+ families. She writes:

"When a family intends to co-feed one baby, this may involve the co-parent inducing lactation or re-lactating. Depending on a family's intentions, the approach of ensuring the birth parent establishes a full supply, given their advantage of having the necessary hormones on their side, tends to be the starting point.

This approach secures the baby's food supply, which is an important ethical consideration. It also allows the co-parent to see what their potential for milk production is via the expressing regime, with or without hormonal assistance, as detailed in the Newman-Goldfarb protocol.

Once both parents are lactating and the baby is 6 weeks old, there can be a balancing of the degree of sharing that the family wish to achieve, while meeting the baby's needs."

A Stor, from a Couple That Co-Fed

Abi and Jordan are gay women who co-fed their two children. Abi writes:

"I gave birth first and I was breastfeeding Olly still when my partner gave birth to our second child, 13 months later. It was a wonderful opportunity to be able to breastfeed both children. This was especially useful, so I was able to support and help my partner, Jordan, those early few weeks, especially when she was unwell following the birth of Freddie. This continued with Jordan being the main breastfeeder for Freddie and I for Olly, but we also both breastfed both children when needed.

They definitely had a preference to breastfeed from the mom who birthed them, which was interesting. We were definitely lucky to be in this situation of both being able to breastfeed our children and we would recommend co-feeding to other LGBTQ+ families. We continued to breastfeed both children until they naturally weaned with Olly being just over 4 years old and Freddie just under 3 years old."

Expressing Milk

Expressing milk means that instead of feeding your baby from the breast/chest, you use your hands or a pump to get milk out. You can exclusively express, or you can combine expressing with feeding at the breast/chest and/or with feeding formula milk. You can also choose to express occasionally or regularly, depending on your situation.

Additionally, you can express during the last month of pregnancy, particularly if you know your baby might need extra milk when first born, or if you simply want to practice. If you have gestational diabetes, for example, you may want to store some milk before birth, because your mature milk might be delayed.

You might need to express if your baby is born prematurely or too unwell to feed directly from you. You could also express to top the baby up, such as if you're trying to prevent or get rid of jaundice. Often, expressing is something you do to keep your milk supply up and to keep the baby fed, with the aim being for you to move towards feeding directly at the source. In a situation involving medical issues, you will probably be given a hospital-grade pump.

Some people also choose to express for other reasons. You may, for instance, have had a traumatic experience that means you do not want someone sucking on you or you may experience gender dysphoria that makes you uncomfortable using your body directly for feeding or having someone close to that part of you. You may also want or need to return to work, so someone else will need to feed your baby while you are occupied.

Whatever the situation, you will need to decide whether to use hand expression or a pump or both. Advice for expressing by hand suggests starting with gentle massage or movement of your breasts/chest. Then, place your "fingers on opposite sides of your areola," "press back toward [the] chest," "compress fingers toward each other, drawing slightly toward nipple but not sliding skin," and then release and repeat (Wiessinger, West, & Pitman, 2013, p. 459).[15]

You can express in the shower or bath, if you just want to practice, but it's hard to save what you express in that case. If you want to save your colostrum (early milk), you might choose to use a syringe or dropper, and if you want to save mature milk, you can express into bowls, bottles, bags, or funnels. Make sure everything is sterilized.

If you decide to use a pump, there are many on the market to choose from. You will want to do some research to see what the different ones have to offer. Some are single pumps, whereas other are double, so you can get both sides done at the same time. There are different noise levels to pumps as well. You will want to think about whether you want to use a battery-operated pump, a hand-operated pump, or a pump that plugs into the wall. Think about where you plan to express and under what circumstances. If you expect to be commuting a lot and will be pumping on a plane or train, a pump that requires a socket won't necessarily be ideal for you. If you will only get a short time to express, a double pump might make sense. You will also find that flange sizes differ, so you may need to buy a few different ones before you find the right size for you.

If you plan to express at work, be sure to check the law in your area and then to talk to your Human Resources department or manager. In the UK, they should provide you with a safe, private

---

15 Sometimes it can be hard to picture physical actions when you just get a verbal description of them. So, if you'd like to see hand expression in action, you can watch this video: "Hand expression of breastmilk" at https://med.stanford.edu/newborns/professional-education/breastfeeding/hand-expressing-milk.html or the videos on the "Droplets" website at https://firstdroplets.com/downloads/ or find others online.

space to pump, breaks in which to express, and a fridge where you can store the milk.

To help you as you express, be warm and comfortable. You can massage your breasts/chest first and you might want to look at photos or videos of your child, or to smell something they've worn. Try not to get stressed about how much milk you get out. When planning expressing sessions, do think about how often you feed your child and how long you'll be apart, so you know how often to express. If you usually feed every two hours, let's say, then you might need to express that often, or perhaps you can comfortably extend the time without feeling engorged or noticing a later drop in supply.

You will need to store the expressed milk safely. As Amy Brown writes, you can store fresh milk in the fridge "for up to five days as long as your fridge is at 4° C or lower" (39° F) and if you want to store it longer than that, put it in the freezer for up to six months (2021, p. 72).

If you find that you have excess expressed milk, you can donate it to other babies (or even adults) in need, or you can use it to help issues such as diaper/nappy rash, cracked nipples, eye infections, and so on. You can even make beautiful jewelry out of it.

Pros and Cons of Expressing Milk

PROS	CONS
You are meeting the nutritional needs of your child.	You will have to express quite regularly, including at night, to keep up with the demand.
Someone else can feed your child while you are working or busy.	You may have to express at work or while otherwise out.

There are many new pumps available now, so you will certainly find one that suits you, or you can hand-express.	You may need to request a private space and/or a mini-fridge so you can express at work.
You can combine expressing with feeding at the breast/chest.	Pumps aren't as efficient as babies and don't stimulate the breast/chest in the same way.

A Stor, About Expressing

Amy, a gender non-conforming butch lesbian, had 7 months of parental leave to care for her child, whom her partner had given birth to. Amy's partner, a bisexual cis woman, expressed milk, which Amy fed to their baby.

Amy describes their situation this way:

"One of the main logistical elements of our leave arrangements was breastfeeding/breastmilk. Our son was given solely breastmilk until he was weaned.

My partner's job involved long days and lots of travel. She has expressed milk the length and breadth of the country! She would take her hand pump and a cool bag with ice blocks with her everywhere and would express whenever she could and whenever she needed to – meetings, train station toilets, in the car. It helped hugely that she works in the women's sector. I would have the electric pump set up for her when she got home in the evenings. She did an amazing job, and I was just so impressed with how she managed everything. We'd bag up and label the milk and store it in the freezer.

I would take our son out in the day with a thermos flask with frozen bags of milk inside, so they could thaw out along the way, or have them warmed up already if we were out on a short trip. My partner breastfed him on they days they were together, and every night.

He never had any trouble having a bottle and breast. I think it was a good bonding experience for all of us.

I felt that one of my main tasks was to make the most of all this milk that my partner was bringing back every day. It was a precious resource, and I wanted to manage it all properly, so I didn't waste any. It required good communication and teamwork. Luckily, those are two things we've always valued in our relationship, and they paid off during those early months of our son's life.

When he went to nursery at 7 months, he continued to be breastfed and bottle-fed with breast milk. We carried on storing milk and dropped it off with him at the nursery every day."

Inducing Lactation

Inducing lactation is a subject that is not well known, even though it has been written about in breastfeeding/chestfeeding contexts for at least 20 years now. Inducing lactation means encouraging the mammary glands of a non-gestational parent to produce milk to feed the baby (or babies). In other words, you do not have to be or have been pregnant in order to lactate.

Induced lactation is a method that can be used in many circumstances. Re-lactating is one form of induced lactation, and it means someone who has lactated before and wants to bring back their milk supply. This can involve feeding subsequent children or someone else's children or even grandchildren. You can also induce lactation to feed a baby that was born by surrogate, to feed an adopted baby or child, or to feed a baby that your partner gestated. It has been employed successfully by an array of women, including trans women.

Unfortunately, this is still considered relatively new, so not all doctors or midwives are familiar with the concept. This means they may not know what medications to prescribe, what approach to suggest, or how best to support you. It also means that you may be treated as a fascinating case study, rather than just as a patient who needs some individualized support.

One way of attempting to induce lactation is to simply put the baby to the breast/chest. This must be done frequently, in order to stimulate the body to begin making milk. This could be a challenge if you have never lactated before and may be frustrating for the baby, who is hungry and getting a chance to suckle but not managing to get milk; this method may work better for someone who is re-lactating. It could be used in combination with a supplemental nursing system (SNS), so the baby does get milk while feeding from you and also can stimulate your milk production at the same time.

The most common way of inducing lactation is probably the Newman-Goldfarb Protocol, which was developed by an IBCLC together with a doctor. When following this protocol, the person typically takes drugs in order to mimic the hormones of pregnancy and birth in their body, so that their body understands that it should lactate. This means you would start with birth control pills and then take domperidone or another drug that is known to have a side effect of causing milk production. After that, you have to regularly use a pump and/or put the baby to the breast/chest to stimulate milk production. Some also recommend taking galactagogues (herbs, medicines, or foods that are supposed to increase milk supply), such as oatmeal or fenugreek. Please note that evidence is mixed on some of these items.

It is usually recommended that you start inducing lactation during the pregnancy or in the lead-up to becoming the baby's guardian, but of course this is not always possible. For example, you may get sudden notice that a child is available for adoption and be given little time to prepare. So, while the earlier the better is a good approach when trying to induce lactation, the protocol can be used at any point.

There have been a few articles published in recent times about both women in a same-sex couple feeding their baby or about trans women feeding babies they could not gestate, and it often seems that inducing lactation gives them a sense of pride and trust in their bodies, as well as a feeling of contributing to the child's emotional and physical wellbeing (Fried, 2017). Even if not much milk is produced through induced lactation, you may find that being able to feed the baby a bit strengthens your bond, helps you feel good about your body and what it can do, and, of course, provides nutrition and comfort to your child.

Pros and Cons of Induced Lactation

PROS	CONS
It can be healing to feed a baby, particularly if you were unable to get pregnant.	Your doctor/midwife may not be familiar with the protocol and may need you to provide them with information.
Two or more parents can share the feeding, each getting a chance to bond or to rest or work as needed.	Depending on where you live, it might be hard to get access to the drugs required. Some doctors may be unwilling to prescribe them for off-label usage.
It can also be affirming to feed a baby at your breast/chest, perhaps especially for trans women.	You may notice changes to your breasts/chest, which you may or may not feel comfortable with.
There is less potential for jealousy about time and emotional involvement with the baby if both or all parents feed.	It may feel risky or like a lot of effort to take drugs and pump frequently.
Since so few people know about induced lactation, it's a chance for you to educate and amaze others.	If both parents are feeding, it may be more challenging for the primary feeding parent to establish their supply, so support is essential.

Advice on Inducing Lactation

Zoe Faulkner, a heterosexual, cisgender IBCLC, has worked with many LGBTQ+ families. Here are her suggestions on inducing lactation:

"For families wanting to induce lactation, there are some excellent resources and books, including Alyssa Schnell's book *Breastfeeding Without Birthing*, which are valuable for these families, including those who have become parents via surrogacy or who wish to induce lactation. Though considerable success can also be achieved via pumping and taking specific herbal galactagogues, there is also the more medicated Newman-Goldfarb protocol to consider.

Supplemental nursing systems are useful tools to provide milk at the breast or chest, often assisting in increasing the milk supply and, importantly, reinforcing the parent-infant feeding relationship."

A Stor, About Inducing Lactation

Amanda, a trans woman, induced lactation. She received support to do this and explains how it worked for her family:

"I'm a trans woman coparenting W, a now 4-year-old child, with Alana, W's birth mother and my long-term partner. Alana and I both nursed W for the first four months of kiddo's life, at which point W started to prefer nursing with Alana, who had a stronger flow. I continued to pump for the next year so that we would be able to supplement Alana's nursing with bottles.

Starting in Alana's first trimester, I began adjusting my hormone levels, taking domperidone, and pumping, in line with a modified Newman-Goldfarb protocol for inducing lactation. By the time W was born, I was making more than

20 oz of milk a day, so was able to nurse our kiddo during the first weeks of W's life, and from that first week, Alana and I were sharing nursing responsibilities.

The experience generally was positive, especially as I had had support both from a lactation consultant and an endocrinologist. It felt meaningful to share the labor of early parenting with Alana in this and many other ways."

Donor Milk

We all know that human milk is the biological norm for human babies, even if it isn't always the cultural norm in all places anymore. However, there are some circumstances when it isn't possible to breastfeed or chestfeed, or when you might not have enough milk. In that case, using donated human milk might be a good approach.

Reasons Why You Might Need Donated Human Milk

You have adopted a baby.
You are a male-male couple (or in a poly male relationship) and don't have breasts or don't wish to lactate.
You are a trans man and you are on hormones and/or have had top surgery.
You have medical reasons that mean you cannot or should not feed.
You have a hormonal or anatomical issue that makes it hard for your body to produce sufficient milk.
You don't want to feed at your chest or express milk but do want to provide human milk.
Your baby is ill or premature and needs more milk than you can provide right now.

If you decide to get donated human milk for your baby, you will need to find it first. This may be done formally. Sometimes, if you're in the hospital or have been in the neonatal intensive care unit (NICU), for example, they will help you with that. They might have donor milk in the hospital, or they might work with a milk bank. You may simply make contact with a milk bank yourself. At a milk bank, they screen the donors and treat the milk so you can be assured that the milk is safe. As Hearts Milk Bank here in the UK writes:

> Donated milk is tested for bacteria, and pasteurized to kill any bacteria or viruses. It is then checked by the laboratory again for any contamination and stored in a temperature-monitored freezer.

They also explain:

> Although donor milk is specially heat-treated to destroy harmful bacteria or viruses, 60% of the antibodies in the milk will survive and be functional to help the baby fight infections; 100% of the special sugars called oligo-saccharides will survive and be functional to help the baby develop a strong immune system. (Both quotes are from HMB FAQ.)

Be aware that there are some milk banks that make a profit and that charge parents (Ruhe, 2015), and that may not be ethical or safe.[16]

The other main option is informal milk sharing. This means you find someone—or multiple people—who is willing to donate to you. There are websites and social media groups and pages dedicated to helping donors and recipients meet up, almost like personal ads. Someone might say where they live, what their diet or lifestyle is like,

---

16 Some adults are even looking for human milk for themselves. Human milk is known to help with some intestinal issues, and also some bodybuilders feel it helps them build their strength. This means that if you donate your milk, some companies/organizations may be making money off it by selling it on to a different audience than you intended. Check to see who you're donating it to.

and how much milk they have and you can decide if this works for you. Alternately, you might write about what you are looking for and a donor might reply. While it is generous of people to offer donor milk, you do also have to recognize that you are going on trust. They may not be honest with their information. For instance, you might prefer someone who is a vegetarian or who does not smoke, but you don't know for sure what the donor does or doesn't do. Also, informal milk sharing has no screening or pasteurizing process, so you may not know if the donor is passing on any bacteria, illnesses, or if the milk has been contaminated or tampered with in any way.

Of course, you can also accept donor milk from a friend or relative. This is potentially safer than informal milk sharing, but it still requires that you trust that your friend or relative keeps the milk stored properly and that they are giving you accurate information about what they consume.

If you get milk informally, you may find that you have to drive long distances to pick up the milk. You may also be asked to cover expenses or to provide storage containers for the milk. If you get it through a milk bank, they may use a courier service to get the frozen milk to your hospital or home.

You will also need to figure out how much milk your baby needs, whether you will combine donor milk with your own milk or with formula milk, and for how long you will want to give the baby donor milk. You will need to store the donor milk safely, which generally means in a freezer.

How to Feed Donated Human Milk to Your Baby

You can use an at-the-breast/chest system (SNS).
You can use a syringe.
You can use a baby spoon.
You can use a bottle.

Pros and Cons of Donor Milk

PROS	CONS
Your baby gets all the benefits of human milk.	It might be tricky to access or track down.
You could enjoy feeding your baby at your chest, if you like.	You might have to pay for it.
If you get the milk from a milk bank, you'll know that the donor and the milk itself has been tested.	If you do informal milk sharing, you have to take it on trust that the people are giving you accurate information.
You can think how lovely it is that some people would donate their excess milk to help others.	You might have to drive long distances frequently in order to pick up the milk.
You get a chance to meet and bond with the parents who share their milk, and maybe their little ones too.	

A Story from a Milk Donor

An anonymous queer woman donated milk informally to several families. She says:

"I was pumping milk when at work, but my child wouldn't drink my expressed milk (they would only breastfeed or drink water), so I ended up with a bit of a freezer stash. I contacted a milk bank and got screened and approved to donate through them, but it turned out that they expected me to pump large amounts for them on a regular basis. I just wasn't able to do that, and they told me it wasn't worth their time to collect my relatively small amounts of milk. So I posted on one of the informal milk-sharing Facebook sites and was able to connect with some families who lived within an hour or two of me.

They came to collect the milk (different families at different times) and it did feel a little awkward, like making small talk with someone on a blind date. I also wished I had some way of proving to them that I didn't smoke or drink or take drugs, but they just had to take my word for it. One family provided me with storage bags to use and another gave me storage bottles. No one paid me and I wouldn't have accepted payment anyway.

I felt happy to be able to help families that wanted to give their children human milk but couldn't. I could see how my own children thrived on my milk, so it made me feel good to know that maybe, in a small way, I could help other children be healthy.

I later found out that human milk is good for adults with stomach problems and is even used as an experimental treatment, so I gave some of my milk to a friend's husband, and also to my own wife, both of whom have IBS. It helped them both.

If I were still pumping milk, I'd definitely donate it again. I did feel disappointed that the formal milk bank hadn't encouraged me more, though."

A Stor, about Milk Donation

Stephanie Wagner, who is herself LGBTQ+, is an IBCLC who specializes in working with LGBTQ+ families. She was contacted for feeding support by two cisgender gay men who used their own sperm, a donor egg, and a gestational carrier. Stephanie has permission to share their story, so here she writes about what their journey was like:

"They contacted me several years ago when they knew their daughter was on the way. At first, at the prenatal home visit when the gestational carrier was about 7 months pregnant, they were just interested in learning about newborn and infant feeding in general, such as how to bottle-feed most effectively, how to mix up artificial infant milk (formula) properly and safely, what to expect with a newborn, how to get sleep; you know, all the things new parents ask professionals who work with babies!

As we started talking, their gestational carrier, who was at the home visit as well, offered to pump her milk after the baby was born so the dads could feed their daughter human milk, if they so desired. The gestational carrier already had had two biological children of her own and had successfully breastfed them each for over a year, so she felt confident in what her milk supply would be after this birth.

The more the dads learned, the more excited they became, and I mentioned how, whether they used human milk or formula, they could still use their bodies/their chests to feed their daughter, if they wanted to. They did not know this was possible but were eager to learn.

I showed them what a supplemental feeding tube was and how to use it, and I worked with the gestational carrier to make sure she was comfortable with the process of exclusively pumping her milk around the clock. I also made sure all three of them knew about proper human milk handling and storage for transporting it from the gestational carrier's home to the dads' home on a regular basis.

The dads included this in their fertility contract and paid the gestational carrier an amount they all agreed upon for her to pump her milk for them after the birth, as that takes time and dedication. The dads' initial goal was to have the gestational carrier pump for one month following the birth, and the dads planned to either chestfeed their daughter with a supplemental feeding tube at their nipple or to bottle-feed their daughter the expressed breast milk provided by the gestational carrier.

The first month went so well for this family that they ended up extending the contract with their gestational carrier, and the gestational carrier continued to pump for 6 months, allowing these two dads, who had no desire to biologically lactate themselves, to still provide exclusive human milk feeds for their daughter for the first 6 months of her life. This is the recommendation made by all leading world parent and baby health organizations, including the World Health Organization (WHO), as the minimum amount of time any baby should receive human milk.

Many of those feeds were done at one of the dads' chests, with their daughter snuggled in their arms, as any cisgender woman who is lactating and breastfeeding would hold her baby. Case scenarios like this one are important for people, especially LGBTQ+ people, to learn about, so they can know that these possibilities exist for their baby and their family too."

Combi-Feeding

Combination-feeding, or combi- or mixed-feeding, is where you combine different feeding methods. You might give your child some human milk—whether from you, your partner, a donor, or some combination thereof—and potentially some formula milk as well.

It may be that you or your partner do not want to feed at the breast/chest or to express, or perhaps not to do those things often, or you may have a low milk supply. For instance, if you induced lactation or if you are on hormones or other medications, it could be that your body does not make as much milk as your baby needs. Perhaps you are using donated human milk but can't get enough of it from your milk bank or informal sharing source. In those cases, and other situations, combining methods might work. It is surprisingly common to mixed-feed, and yet those who do so report feeling invisible or embarrassed, or they don't know where to go for accurate information on how to go about it (Ruddle, 2021).

If you combi-feed, you would know that your baby is still getting the benefit of some human milk and possibly still having the physical bonding with you or your partner if feeding at the breast/chest, while also being certain that there is enough for the baby to eat.

Pros and Cons of Combi-Feeding

PROS	CONS
Your baby gets some human milk, which is the optimum source of nutrition.	You may need to track down sources of human milk and/or formula.
You still get to bond while feeding your baby.	You may have expenses related to donated milk and/or formula.
You may experience some psychological or emotional relief if your baby is not wholly dependent on your milk supply.	There are some risks involved in feeding formula or informally shared milk.

A Story from Someone Who Combination-Fed

Earlier in this book, Ellen and Rhiannon shared their story of using an unknown donor's sperm and Rhiannon's eggs to make their babies. Ellen carried their younger two children and combi-fed them. Ellen describes their feeding journey:

"The twins were bottle-fed. They were 5 weeks early, born by planned C-section as Georgia wasn't growing well. Georgia went straight into NICU, and I expressed for her. Joseph stayed with me, and I breastfed him. He lost over 12% of his body weight and I realized my milk never came in.

I was advised to bottle-feed. I chose to continue expressing for them both and to top up with formula. I got a prescription for a drug that was supposed to help milk production and tried eating special cookies that were supposed to help but I just couldn't produce the amount of milk they needed.

I was never offered lactation support (the three of us were in NICU for 2 weeks).

It didn't help that they both had tongue-tie (which was picked up privately weeks later) so had struggled to feed anyway. I continued to express for 6 weeks mainly in the hope more milk would come and to give the twins the benefits of breast milk. Georgia was still a low weight, so if she were breastfed, it would be hard to know how much she was taking in. The lack of sleep, the stress, and the need for Georgia to gain weight caused me to decide to fully bottle-feed, after this initial period of combi-feeding."

Another Combination-Feeding Story

Kat and her wife, both lesbians, combi-fed both their children. Kat writes:

"With our first child, my wife initially tried to breastfeed, but it didn't go very well. She persevered, but we needed to supplement with formula while she pumped milk that we also gave to the baby.

We found, as a result, that we felt like we both had a more even bond with the baby, so when I became pregnant with baby two, we made the conscious choice to combination-feed from the outset.

Baby two had no issues breastfeeding, but we were careful to make sure she didn't get too much of one or the other and felt comfortable and able to switch between.

As a result, we both feel like we have had strong bonds with both children from the outset, and also, that we were both able to share the burden of night feeds and feeding while out, etc. It worked well for us.

I think being LGBTQ+ made us more open to this method
in the first place, and it helped that we birthed one each.
But there's no reason this wouldn't work equally well for a
straight couple."

Formula-Feeding

Formula-feeding means exclusively giving a baby non-human
milk, nearly always made from cows' milk and sometimes from soy.
While there is no doubt that human milk is what human babies
need, formula milk will suffice. It is important to know that there
are well-documented risks involved in feeding a baby formula, but
that sometimes people must make this choice or prefer to make
this choice. Be aware that many Western countries have a strong
preference for formula-feeding (think of all the times someone
breastfeeding/chestfeeding is told to cover up or to go elsewhere
to do it), and that you may be influenced by these negative attitudes, so be sure you are making the choice that resonates most
strongly with your needs and your innermost beliefs and desires.
As mentioned earlier, it is known that people can feel grief about
not feeding their babies directly with their bodies (Brown, 2019), so
think about whether you are choosing formula because it's truly
right for you or whether you have been pressured by your family,
friends, or societal messages to do so.

There are lots of reasons why you might decide formula is your
way forward. You might be a male-male (or poly male) couple with
no ability or desire to lactate and no chance of getting donor milk,
or if you are trans or non-binary, you might find it too dysphoric to
feed. You might just not want to. Perhaps this is due to trauma or
uncomfortable feelings, or you may simply feel that breastfeeding/
chestfeeding is something you do not want to do. Whatever the
situation, how you feed your baby is up to you, and you don't have
to defend or explain yourself.

Oh, and just so you know, research shows that, basically, all
formulas are the same, because there are requirements about what
they should be composed of (see First Steps Nutrition, 2021 for more

on this). So don't be swayed by the fancy advertising or the different slogans or claims. You could pick any container of formula off the shelf and feel confident that it contains what's legally mandated for formula. All you need to do is to make it up according to the instructions. You aren't depriving your child if you don't buy the super-expensive, organic, omega-3-filled formula that will supposedly make your little one the next Nobel Prize-winner.

Pros and Cons of Formula-Feeding

PROS	CONS
If you cannot or do not want to feed from your body, your baby will still get fed.	You may feel defensive or shamed about your choice.
Formula is widely available.	You may feel tempted to spend lots of money on special formula.
Some people like sharing bottle-feeds with partners, relatives, or friends.	You need to be sure you follow the instructions for mixing and storing formula.
	Formula is, unfortunately, missing many of the key ingredients of human milk.

A Story About Formula-Feeding

Kay and Lauren, a lesbian couple, have one child. Kay writes:

"I decided as the birth mother to formula-feed so that my wife could also feed him, and it wasn't all down to me.

Another reason for me choosing this way is due to feeding time being the perfect time for bonding. I didn't want my wife to miss out on this experience.

I'm so pleased this is the way we chose to feed our child, as we discovered he had a milk protein allergy, so really, it was a blessing in disguise.

Just because I birthed him doesn't mean he's any less of my wife's son. People have many views on this. But he's *our* little boy, and it's lucky we know other children who have same-sex parents,so they can relate to one another as they grow up."

Another Stor , About Formula-Feeding

Francis, a queer trans man, is a single father who gestated his child and chose to use formula because of his gender dysphoria. He describes his journey as follows:

"I have wanted kids for as long as I can remember. When I started testosterone, the gender clinic told me that it would make me infertile. A couple of years later, I found a Facebook group for trans and non-binary gestational parents and learned that this is not true; fertility returns to what it would be without testosterone.

I decided to come off testosterone and try to conceive with the aid of IVF and donor sperm. I was and still am single and had reached an age where I didn't want to wait any longer. The IVF worked on the first attempt! So I am now a single gestational father.

When I decided to try to conceive, I waited to come off testosterone until a month after top surgery. I knew I wouldn't cope with the dysphoria during pregnancy.

I knew that some people can chestfeed in a supplemental way, but I decided to use formula exclusively to avoid the associated dysphoria. There was a certain sadness as I worried that I would be letting my baby down.

After my baby's birth, my body produced a little milk and I had brief second thoughts. I talked to my obstetrician about it and realized chestfeeding was not a viable option for me because of the dysphoria involved. My baby is healthy and happy. We have a close bond and I have no regrets about exclusively bottle-feeding."

A Few Other Things About Feeding

There are some other useful and interesting things to know when it comes to feeding your baby.

First of all, as has become clear in this section, there are many approaches to feeding, and you will find one or more ways that work best for you, your baby, and your specific situation. In addition, there are often new developments, new tools, or new research findings that can be valuable. Stephanie Wagner, an LGBTQ+ IBCLC, says,

> There are lots of other tools, such as nipple shields, nipple evertors, nipple shells, milk pumps, milk collectors, as well as foods, herbs, medications, among other things, that we can use in our field to help a parent reach their goals around feeding their baby. With more advances happening in healthcare and LGBTQ+ medicine in general, the possibilities are always changing and that is exciting and necessary for all of us who are LGBTQ+ (personal communication, 2021).

The more of us who are out and open about our families, the more doctors and researchers will learn, and this, in turn, will lead to further advances that will benefit us all.

Non-Induced Lactation

Another thing you might like to know is the somewhat surprising news that non-induced lactation can happen. This means that someone who has not gestated or given birth to a baby can suddenly find themselves lactating. It's thought that the hormone rush that comes with having a new baby can make the non-gestational parent lactate. One person I spoke with told me that they had had no idea it could happen, until it suddenly did. A midwife told her that she could encourage the milk by expressing, but in the end, this person chose not to do that. It is exciting to think about what our bodies can do. If you do find yourself lactating despite not having given birth or tried to induce lactation, and if you want to increase your milk production so you could contribute to feeding your baby, get support from a midwife or lactation consultant right away. You'll want to express frequently to increase your production and you may also choose to use drugs the way someone who chose to induce lactation does.

Breastfeeding Agitation and Aversion

An additional important topic is breastfeeding aversion. Technically called breastfeeding agitation and aversion (BAA), this is where the feeding parent finds it physically, emotionally, and/or mentally difficult to feed. This can start at birth or develop when a child gets older. It can be situational, such as someone finding feeding unpleasant or uncomfortable when they are menstruating, or it can be all the time. Some people find that they have aversion with one child but not another. This can be incredibly upsetting, painful, and/or confusing. If you get aversion, you might find that your skin feels itchy or even crawls while you are feeding. You might want to throw your child across the room or hit your child (obviously, though, please don't actually do that). You could feel rage, sadness, guilt, or shame. You might want to unlatch your child or get away from them. It's okay to feel these things. You don't need to blame yourself for them; they are normal and more common than we let on. BAA is not something most people want and, in fact, most feeding parents who experience BAA still want to continue feeding.

So, what can you do if you are struck with BAA? First of all, take care of yourself. Stay hydrated and well fed, get plenty of rest (I know that seems laughable if you've got a child), try taking magnesium (which many people find helpful), and join a supportive group (there are several on social media, for example). Then think about how you can make feeding easier.

Common techniques including setting boundaries around feeding and limiting how often it happens and/or where it takes place. You can tell your child you'll only feed for the length of a particular song, or while you count to a certain number. You can try distracting yourself by watching TV or a movie, or reading a book while feeding, so you don't feel as conscious of the intrusive thoughts or emotions, or you can use meditation or mindfulness to help you calm down. You can try distracting your child, so they don't want to feed as often.

As with the other challenging issues mentioned in this book, you can also look to support from a lactation consultant or a therapist. If it's bad, you can think about weaning; this doesn't have to be complete weaning, because you might find that there are particular times of the day when you experience the aversion less or at least enjoy feeding more, so you could keep those and drop some of the others. Whatever you do, just remember that you aren't alone in experiencing this and having BAA doesn't make you a bad parent (Yate, 2020).

Tandem-Feeding

Finally, let's discuss tandem-feeding. I mentioned it above, in the section that was generally on breastfeeding. It means feeding two or more children at the same time (though I've also seen some people call themselves tandem-feeders when they feed one child while pregnant with the next). Yes, your body is capable of producing enough milk for more than one child. Amazing, isn't it? Humans wouldn't ever produce twins, triplets, or other multiples if we couldn't nurture them, and we wouldn't be able to continue feeding through pregnancy if it were too much for our bodies. So, if some "helpful" (read: interfering) midwife or doctor tells you that you're depriving your growing fetus of nutrients while still feeding another child or that you are doing your baby a disservice by also feeding the baby's older sibling (or even siblings), know that this isn't true. By the way, breastfeeding aversion can happen when you're tandem-feeding, so you might feel agitated feeding your older child but not the younger one, or vice versa. There are ways around this; some of them were suggested above.

Tandem-feeding can be a fantastic way of creating a bond between your older child and your new baby (seeing them hold hands or stroke each other across your body can be so moving), so you might like trying it to see what happens, but if it doesn't work to feed them at the same time, or if you have BAA while doing so, you could consider feeding them separately. In that case, you'll need to give priority to the baby, who will be more dependent on you.

A Story About Tandem-Feeding and More

Earlier in this book, Nicki and Anna, a gay couple, wrote about their experience with fertility treatment and surrogacy. Nicki carried their first two children, and a surrogate carried their third.

Nicki was still breastfeeding their second child when the third one was born, and she tandem-fed the two younger ones. But their feeding story also includes expressing, formula-feeding, tongue-tie, and getting support. Nicki writes:

"Perhaps the biggest challenge we encountered was breast-feeding. One of the main reasons we went ahead with surrogacy as quickly as we did after the birth of our second child was so that I could breastfeed. When Elin was born, Andrew was 23 months old and still nursing, which meant that I had a milk supply in order to feed her.

Breastfeeding was important to me with both the boys, but it was even more important to me with Elin. I think this was because I felt that I had no genetic link but also, unlike with the boys, I had no physical link from being pregnant with her. Breastfeeding was the one thing that I could do for her.

I began pumping on top of nursing Andrew when Jamielee,

our surrogate, was about 7 months pregnant. I received massively varying advice about this. I spoke to two different lactation consultants and the hospital breastfeeding specialist, and one told me I should be pumping eight times a day, including overnight, one said to pump as and when I could, and the third told me that I didn't need to do anything at all, as the baby would stimulate supply when she arrived. I opted for the middle option.

Anna was deployed with work and so I was solo parenting for the last 8 weeks of the pregnancy. It was impossible to find the time to pump eight times a day and keep the household running and the boys cared for. I definitely increased the volume of milk I was producing, and Andrew thought this was great and increased the amount he was nursing in response. When Elin was born, she latched shortly afterwards and that was such a special feeling.

Jamielee expressed colostrum for us so that Elin didn't miss out, as I was unable to produce that. Unfortunately, we had so many challenges with our breastfeeding journey.

Elin had a tongue-tie[17], which we had snipped when she was 3 weeks old and failing to gain weight. We had to give top-ups of breastmilk to try to get her to gain weight and were then referred to a pediatrician, who pushed us to switch to formula.

Elin was an unsettled and miserable newborn. She had reflux, was frequently sick, and was obviously in pain. She screamed and screamed for hours, and we felt something

---

17 A tongue-tie is a "restricted lingual frenulum" (Oakley, 2021, p. 18). This is when the membrane attached to the tongue is too tight or does not move as much as it ideally would, which makes it difficult for the child to open their mouth wide and for the tongue to create negative pressure on the breast/chest. Some tongue-ties can be cut, removing the restriction. If you suspect there is a tongue-tie, get support immediately, as it can impact feeding, regardless of your feeding method.

was significantly wrong. Despite not wanting to, we did start giving her formula as well as breastfeeding, but she then developed a bottle preference and refused to nurse. I was devastated but was advised to try using a supplemental nursing system (SNS) to feed Elin formula at the breast. This was a real challenge to use, and even more awkward to wash, and I hated it initially. Elin still wasn't gaining weight well and was still utterly miserable.

Eventually, we were admitted to the hospital and forced to switch exclusively to formula while I pumped to keep my supply up, as I was not prepared to give up. On specialist allergy formula, Elin was a different baby and we then set out to work out what she was reacting to. Eventually, we figured out that she was reacting to dairy, soya, eggs, prawns, mango, pineapple, and grapes through my milk. I cut out these things and we gradually reduced the amount of formula she received through the SNS.

Finally, she began putting on weight properly and, much to our relief, was so much happier. The SNS was a real blessing to me. I am certain we would not have got Elin back to the breast without it.

I feel that our breastfeeding journey suffered hugely due to a lack of knowledge and support, and the push for formula. Time after time, medical professionals insisted that her lack of weight gain was due to my milk being 'toddler milk' and not suitable for a baby. Simultaneously, the lactation consultant I saw privately kept insisting that this was not true. I was caught in the middle and my mental health crumbled as I tried to work out what to do for the best.

I do understand that our situation was unusual, but I had to explain to multiple medical professionals how I was able to breastfeed when I had not given birth to our baby. Breastfeeding was never the source of comfort and the fix-all that it was for the boys, but I am glad that Elin continued to get the many health benefits of breastmilk until she self-weaned at 11 months. I will continue to nurse Andrew until he self-weans, whenever that may be!"

Another Tandem-Feeding Stor,

Miriam, a lesbian, has two children with her wife. Miriam writes:

"I have loved breastfeeding, so I was excited about the idea of tandem-feeding, but it ended up a lot more complicated than I'd expected.

First, because I was still breastfeeding my older child when I wanted to get pregnant again, I had to deal with the fertility clinic. They refused to treat me if I was still feeding, so I had to wait a while and then pretend that I'd stopped feeding.

But that meant it was all on me to make sure the drugs they prescribed me were safe for my older child. I did a lot of research! I also asked for lower doses of drugs, to try to ensure my milk supply wasn't affected too much. Throughout the fertility treatment, I did experience a small dip in supply, as well as some real pain and aversion when feeding, but I carried on.

It took several attempts at IUI and two full rounds of IVF before I got pregnant with our second child.

Then, I was ill during pregnancy, which made continuing to breastfeed a challenge too. Still, I kept at it. I didn't want to wean my older child when they weren't ready.

Finally, I had our younger child. Tandem-feeding wasn't always as easy or as beautiful as I'd imagined. There was some jealousy from the older child. Finding comfortable positions wasn't straightforward. And I felt some aversion about feeding the older one, possibly because their latch wasn't as good as it had previously been.

In the end, I usually fed the children separately. Then there'd be some amazing times, like when I'd manage to latch them

both on and I'd be cuddling them both, and they'd be holding hands, and it felt so good. I felt so connected to them
and I could sense their connection too.

I do think that continuing to feed the older child helped
with their transition to becoming a big sibling and it helped
cement the bond between the two children.

I was also proud that my body was able to do it, despite the
fertility treatment, the illness, the aversion, and the pain. I
tandem-fed for around 2 years."

Conclusion

As is clear from the foregoing sections, there are many possible ways
of feeding babies. Perhaps we could even claim that there are more
options for LGBTQ+ parents than there are for non-LGBTQ+ people.
You need to choose the right method or methods for yourself, your
baby, and your situation.

What I think is a key message from many of these stories is
the importance of getting support. Breastfeeding/chestfeeding is
generally possible for most people, but sometimes it doesn't feel
that way because of circumstances. Getting to a support group or
seeing a lactation consultant or breastfeeding counsellor can be the
difference between continuing to feed from your body or feeling
like you want or need to give up.

In general, when it comes to how you feed your baby, as with
how you make your family, try to inform yourself as much as possible so you can make the decision that feels right for you and for
your family.

Supporting LGBTQ+ Families

Information for Allies and Healthcare Professionals

The earlier sections of this book were aimed primarily at LGBTQ+ people, but they also contained information that would be useful for those who work with or who are in solidarity with LGBTQ+ folks. This chapter, however, is intended specifically for the professionals and allies, because I recognize that it isn't always a simple matter to know what to say or do when faced with a situation you haven't previously come across. You might feel awkward or uncomfortable or worry about doing the wrong thing.

I have a few tips just for you, although I also want to emphasize that actually, simply trying to learn more and to be a little more inclusive is a huge step that is to be applauded. We can all do better in many areas of our professional and personal lives, and having good intentions and educating ourselves is the first thing we can try to do.

In fact, it often isn't as hard to be inclusive and welcoming as we sometimes assume. Basically, my suggestions can be summed up as "be respectful and kind." That's just good advice for life, don't you think? In a bit more detail: think carefully about what words we use in which situations, reconsider our assumptions about certain topics, be cautious about asking questions, continue to learn and grow, and gain an awareness of specific medical, emotional, and practical issues that impact LGBTQ+ people. We can do that, right?

Terminology

I referred to terminology in general earlier in this book and how the acronym LGBTQ+ can cover a wide range of identities and I also talked about the names LGBTQ+ parents might be called by their children, but here, I want to specifically focus on ways that allies and healthcare professionals can be supportive of LGBTQ+ people by using appropriate language. Using the word, pronoun, term, or title that your client employs shows them respect and consideration. Sometimes, this may require a slight shift in your perspective. For example, you may usually consider everyone giving birth to be a "woman" and a "mummy" or "mommy," and might have to accept that not everyone feels that those words apply to them. It's not any harder than, say, pronouncing someone's name correctly or calling them by their nickname, if that's what they prefer.

Recently, Brighton and Sussex University Hospitals National Health Service Trust in the UK produced new guidelines that suggested that midwives, doctors and others working with birthing people consider using certain words, such as "human milk" (Green & Riddington, 2021). This attracted some controversy (British Broadcasting Service, 2021), but the people who got upset by the new guidelines missed the point. We aren't demanding that you use terms for yourself that feel wrong—if you are happy to say you are a woman who breastfeeds, then that's what's right for you—instead, we're simply saying that you should be aware that other people might use other terms, and it doesn't do you any harm to talk to someone about their chestfeeding. It's adding terminology, not taking it away. Plus, it expands our minds and hearts when we learn new words and concepts.

Similarly, if you can make changes to where you work or volunteer that would make language usage more inclusive, that could be hugely meaningful to those you serve. For example, the maternity unit could perhaps be called the perinatal unit, gestational unit, parental center, or birthing center. A breastfeeding or mother-and-baby group could be called a feeding support group or a parent-and-baby group. There are many ways of ensuring that everyone feels included from the first moment, and the easiest place to start is with the title of the service or activity. Research on transmasculine parents notes,

> Care providers and others are capable of *causing* gender dysphoria in a patient by misgendering them. Conversely, care providers can affirm a patient's gender

identity through appropriate language, respectful touch, and other intentional actions, and thus alleviate distress associated with gender dysphoria (MacDonald et al., 2016).

This concept—that care providers can cause harm or, alternatively, that they can affirm the identity of the people they are working with—is important to remember; every word we speak matters.

On a more individual level, it perhaps sounds obvious to say that your language should reflect the language that the person you are working with uses. If you aren't sure, ask. Most people won't take offense if you say, "My name is X, and my pronouns are such-and-such. What are yours?" Few people would be upset if you ask, "So, who do we have here today?" On the contrary, they'll be thrilled that you're making the effort. By asking, you are showing that you care enough to get it right, and you're leaving it open for people to tell you their own story.

Traditionally, we assumed that a pregnant or birthing person is a woman and that her partner would necessarily be a man. Of course, we now recognize that this isn't always the case. Throughout human history, there have always been many possible family set-ups, even if they weren't labelled as LGBTQ+ specifically. These days, you might have people who describe themselves as the gestational or non-gestational parent, the birthing or non-birthing parent, the nursing or feeding parent or the non feeding parent. Some might just say parent, or pare or par for short, while others choose to use gendered words such as mum/mom, mama, mother, dad, daddy, papa, or father. Some people use words from other languages or employ their first names, either alone or in combination with another word, such as Pat or Mama Pat or Ima[18] Pat. Others use gender-neutral parental terms, such as poppy or dom.

---

18 Hebrew for mother.

Be careful about assuming that parents come in the one-man, one-woman format. For instance, if you are running an antenatal class, don't separate people up into groups called "the moms" and "the dads." In general, for example, not all groups of women like being referred to as "ladies" or "mommies." They may not identify with those words, even if they do think of themselves as women.

Along the same lines, two people in a relationship do not necessarily identify as a husband and wife, although some do. They could be partners, boyfriends, girlfriends, coparents, spouses, significant others, or more. I've heard people talk about their husbutch, companion, or boifriend, among other terms. If two women come to an appointment with you as the midwife, don't ask if one is the sister, mother, aunt, or friend of the pregnant one. Let them tell you about who they are and what their relationship is.

Along with terms to describe themselves and their relationships, remember that today, more people are choosing pronouns that may be different from what you would expect. Not all people giving birth call themselves she. Besides she, there's he, they, e, ey, xe, ze, ne, and more. Offering your own pronouns, whether orally or on your ID badge or in your email signature, might make people feel more comfortable telling you theirs.

In terms of titles, many people seem to believe that women are either Miss or Mrs. while men are Mr., but of course, there is also Ms., Mx., Dr., Professor, and many other possible titles. It is common for doctors to introduce themselves as Dr. X and then to use the client's or patient's first name, but that suggests an imbalance of power and a lack of equality. That sort of patronizing language disparity may also contribute to people feeling disempowered and unable to say how they identify or what they want to happen in a medical setting. For that reason, I would recommend using first names for everyone or titles for everyone, unless the patient/client suggests something else.

Terminology extends beyond how people identify to the ways they form their families and raise their children. If people use a sperm or egg donor, the donor is often not the father or mother, unless that is the word that that particular family chooses to employ. A donor contributes biological material and genetic information but is usually not involved in the raising of the child. Some people do use a known sperm donor and they might call the donor the father or the uncle, or they might use the donor's first name, while many other people choose to allow their children to decide on terms, if and when they want to.

I have already mentioned that not all people feel comfortable using words such as breastfeeding or breast milk, because of the gendered implications of the word breast, so offering other options, such as chestfeeding, nursing, feeding, body feeding, or human milk can make clients feel more accepted.

Besides doing this in speaking, it is worth looking at the forms you use at work or the way you keep notes on clients. Instead of having forms that ask for the mother's and father's medical information, why not write parents' medical information? That would work for many, perhaps most, people. If you must use the form, don't simply run through word-for-word it with each client but rather carefully pick which sections to use or which words to employ or adapt it as necessary. See the earlier section in this book on the emotional pain paperwork can inflict. Try to treat each client you meet as an individual, rather than either as just as everyone else you meet or as a cool new case to analyze. If you do this, your paperwork and consultations will feel more inclusive.

In short, there is a huge amount of variety in terms of how people identify and what terms or pronouns they use for describing themselves, their relationships, and their experiences as parents. All we have to do is let people tell us what words to use and then reflect those words back at them. It shows that you esteem and care for people by ensuring you describe them as they want to be described. Remember, you probably don't want to be called by the wrong name or pronoun either.

What Are Your Own Terms?

What pronouns do you use? Why?
What name do you want people to call you? Is it the same name you were given at birth?
What terms best describe your roles in life? Would you feel comfortable correcting someone who got them wrong?
How do you introduce yourself to people? What's important for them to understand about you?

A Stor About Terminolog

Kaedan, a genderqueer/non-binary person who birthed and nursed both their children, is partnered with a cis man.

Kaedan experienced being misgendered during labor and also came to realize how much medical professionals gender babies and children, even when asked not to. Here, Kaedan writes about terminology and what medical professionals might do differently:

"One thing that stands out about the second birth is that when we transferred to the hospital from home, clearly the staff had been given an anti-bias or diversity training around gender and caring for gender non-conforming/trans patients, because the first thing they did once I got to my room was confirm my preferred name (different from my legal name in their system) and that my pronouns were they/them (listed in a note in their system).

What was so funny is that even though I confirmed that my pronouns were they/them, whenever the nurse would change shifts and get the incoming nurse up to speed with my birth, they would go like, "Okay, this is Kaedan who uses they/them pronouns. She is fully dilated, and she has been pushing for 3 hours," etc. They totally lost the pronoun once it was out of the context of the initial confirmation.

I personally am not too attached to my pronouns, and I was in so much pain that I didn't care in that instance, but for many other people, being misgendered in that way could have been distressing and could have distracted them from the important work of labor. For instance, luckily, they never used my legal name while I was in labor, but if they had, that totally would have messed with my head and possibly interfered with how my body progressed in labor. I wish healthcare professionals would understand that respecting and seeing someone's gender isn't just a "preference" or the PC-thing to do—it could make the difference between a vaginal birth and a C-section, or an empowered versus a traumatic birth.

Also, I wish the practice in hospital everywhere would be to never, ever, ever announce the sex of a child until the parents ask or look themselves. We spent so much energy remembering to tell this to the hospital staff when we first came in and then at every shift change. We had it in our birth plan, but we didn't necessarily trust that the staff would remember or had read it, so it was something we were concerned about because it was important to us to have the first several minutes after birth just soaking in this new little person without any knowledge of their sex—just getting to know them for them without a conditioned response around sex/gender. Maybe they wouldn't have said anything but given that it was often a surprise during ultrasounds that we didn't want to know the sex during pregnancy, it seemed like it was often one of the first things the staff person would say upon delivery.

For both of our children, we also used they/them from birth and, in many instances, didn't share their sex with people, so as to avoid our kids being immediately gendered based on their sex and to give them space to explore their gender on their terms. This was a constant point of education for hospital staff during the labor and in our hospital stay, not to mention at later pediatric appointments.

At my older child's 4-year check-up, for instance, at which the doctor asked them a series of questions to test their development, they asked my kid, "Are you a boy or a girl?" Because the doctor knew we were raising them gender-neutral or gender-creatively, she then quickly added, "Or neither/something else?" She then reflected aloud how this is a typical developmental check-in question for this age to see if they are developing a sense of self and able to categorize things in their mind, but that she was realizing the problematic nature of only having the two binary options available for kids to choose from.

Luckily, given that we live in a queer-friendly place with a fairly high percentage of the population aware and/ or educated about LGBTQ issues, this type of parenting choice isn't completely unknown to people, but I imagine it could feel a lot more foreign/isolating in other parts of the country/world.

Becoming a parent has made me want to be braver in correcting people when they misgender me, partly for myself but also so I can model for my kids how this can be done so they see it and can get more confident in correcting people if they themselves are misgendered.

Giving my kids the space to explore their gender and gender expression has also opened up more space within myself to explore more. For instance, pre-kids, I think I felt more pressure to express a certain "queer esthetic" so that I could signal to people that I was queer. In some ways, being visible in this way mattered less to me as I got older, but in other ways, I think I allowed myself to step back and reflect on what forms of expression feel comfortable to me and truly bring me joy, as opposed to wearing certain clothes or keeping a certain hairstyle because it's what I saw other queer people wear.

Finding that framing of gender expression as the things that brings you joy and make you feel the most confident was a real game-changer. It seems so obvious looking back on it now but emphasizing joy and confidence in identity choices was never something that was offered to or spelled out for me. It feels wonderful to get to offer that to my kids, and to gain more confidence in myself through this process."

Developing Terminology

Stephanie Wagner is an LGBTQ+ registered nurse and IBCLC who runs EverLatching Love (www.everlatchinglove.com), which provides breastfeeding, chestfeeding, and body-feeding support and education. Making sure healthcare is always aware of diversity, equity, and inclusion for all people is a pillar of Steph's approach, and she has been featured on TV and across the media for her activism and work.

Steph works with many LGBTQ+ families and here she describes how terminology can develop and why it is important that it does so:

"I did not necessarily set out in private practice to also become a representative for LGBTQ+ parents and families. I am open about who I am as a person and have always made it clear on my website and business messaging that I am a healthcare professional who is inclusive of all persons and families and who stands in the principle of DEI (diversity, equity, and inclusion) healthcare as much as possible. Slowly, over time, more and more LGBTQ+ families started reaching out to me.

It was, is, and always will be an honor to work with folx in our community. More and more, I kept hearing LGBTQ+ clients talk about the language we use in our profession and in medicine in general and how it does not fit them: doesn't fit their identity, their orientation, their anatomy, and/or family.

Chestfeeding and bodyfeeding are inclusive descriptive terms and actions that many LGBTQ+ parents find more suitable to use to explain how they feel about their body/identity/orientation as a non-heteronormative parent who is feeding their baby. I now use breastfeeding/chestfeeding/bodyfeeding, all three words, as the way I talk about the work that I do, as all parents deserve a seat at the baby feeding table, and there is plenty of room for all parents.

I see inclusive healthcare and medicine as not only a necessity, but a lifeline, for so many. The beauty of all of us challenging ourselves in medicine to rethink the language we use, to rethink the way we were taught to assess other people and bodies, and to even unlearn some things we were originally taught, is that it does not exclude anyone else. No one should get left behind in medicine, because healthcare, I feel, is a human right.

Regardless of how any one person identifies, we are all still human beings. In the breastfeeding/chestfeeding/bodyfeeding field, we work with human parents having human babies, and *all* babies deserve the chance to be fed with human milk."

Assumptions

The foregoing section on terminology had the message that we cannot make assumptions about who people are, what their relationships look like, and what words they want us to use. In general, we all need to think through what ideas we have about family creation, gender roles, parenthood, and so on, and to consider how scientific and medical advances and legal rights have changed things. We need to be cautious about assuming we know anything about the individual, couple, throuple, or family in front of us.

In all my years of work supporting families, one of the most common assumptions I've come across is one that particularly affects heterosexual, cisgender families. This is the belief that men are useless and unable to contribute to taking care of children. I've repeatedly been told that men cannot put a diaper/nappy or clothes on the baby, soothe the baby, or entertain or teach older children, among other such stereotyped ideas. It doesn't seem fair to limit someone's involvement because of outdated beliefs about their gender. Similarly, we should be careful about making assumptions based on someone's class, sexuality, ethnicity, ability, religion, and other characteristics.

Just because someone has certain body parts or has participated in a particular way in the making or feeding of a baby does not mean that their gender identity or sexuality is a foregone conclusion. For example, a parent who did not give birth is not necessarily a father or a man. A non-birth mother is still a mother (if they use the term mother). A trans man would, in most cases, not want to be viewed as a mother (if someone is a man, then they might feel that the word father describes them best). A parent who is breastfeeding or chestfeeding does not necessarily identify as a woman or a mother. Then again, they might do. As ever, listening to people and asking questions if you aren't sure is the way to show that you care enough to try to get it right. Just be cautious about the words you use when asking. If you have two women in your office, you probably don't want to ask, "Who's the dad of this baby?" If you are working with a trans man, you most likely don't want to start your interaction by saying, "So, Mommy, how are you enjoying motherhood?"

What Assumptions Do You Have?

When you think about what a family looks like, what comes to mind?
What do you think a woman looks like and does? What about a man?
What do you think about LGBTQ+ people? What rights do you think they should have?
What is a mother? What is a father?

| What tasks are involved in caring for a baby and who should do them and why? |
| What do you think is different, if anything, about how LGBTQ+ people might make their families or raise their children? |
| What values do you think LGBTQ+ people might have and how might this impact their parenting? |

Another Word About Assumptions

By the way, it isn't just your clients you might make assumptions about; you might also have certain ideas about your fellow professionals. For example, there's an idea that doctors are men and nurses are women. You might think that all midwives or doulas must be people who have had children themselves. This isn't always the case and sometimes we have to be careful about what we say to those we're working with. It can be painful if you ask someone about their children, only to find out that perhaps they wanted a baby, but it didn't work out. Not only can that hurt the person you're talking to, but it can also make them feel as though you're questioning their competence. Do you think someone has to be a parent in order to work with parents? Does someone have to be LGBTQ+ to support LGBTQ+ people?

I've experienced this issue myself, in lots of areas of my personal and professional life. When I was starting out as a queer woman as a breastfeeding counsellor—later, a lactation consultant—and also as a doula, I had a real concern that clients and other professionals might not want to work with me. I was worried that they might think I had gone into this career because I liked looking at women's bodies. In other words, society has so sexualized women's bodies that even though I simply wanted to support people with birth and infant feeding, I was nervous about how others might perceive my intentions. I mean, I'm sure there are people out there who see a laboring or lactating body as sexual, but that isn't at all how it is for me. I also discovered that there was an assumption that religious people wouldn't want to work with me, because they wouldn't approve of who I was. In fact, several times, I was asked if I was available to work with some clients, only to be told, "Oh, wait, they're religious. Maybe it's better if we recommend someone else to them." It seemed sad that they might miss out on my expertise because of either their beliefs and their assumptions about me, or because of someone else's assumptions about the potential client's assumptions (if you can follow that. Basically, we made assumptions about assumptions, like a particularly hard game of Telephone/Whispers). Likewise, when I have gone to see clients who were described as religious, I was apprehensive, even though I needn't have been, because they wouldn't have hired me if they didn't want to work with me.

I'm not the only one who's experienced this. So, let's all be careful about what we assume about one another. We can learn a lot from each other if we're careful to remember that we're all individuals.

A Stor, About Assumptions

Rachel Priestly is a gay woman who is also an IBCLC (see https://rachelpriestley-ibclc.co.uk/). When she was first looking to enter the profession, she was surprised to find that it was her own then-partner who thought it was wrong for an LGBTQ+ person to become an IBCLC. But Rachel pressed on, realizing how important it was for there to be queer lactation consultants.

Rachel remembers her partner saying, "I always thought it was a bit off. You wanting to work with women and be up close to their boobs all day. There's something not right about that. Disgusting, really."

Rachel adds:

"Those words uttered near to the beginning of my career represented the dying embers of a fire that had raged through my relationship with my then-girlfriend, one filled with pain, control, and submission, and they rang in my ears as I walked through what felt like a career minefield of other people's potentially explosive opinions. Conversations at work had to be carefully navigated just in case—woven through with awkwardly inserted gender-neutral pronouns, barely obscuring a fearful bid to avoid outing my little family and risking blowing my career and our sole income out of the water.

My fears about my abusive partner's assertion that being a gay lactation consultant would be seen as dodgy hung around for a long time but wanting other queer families to feel represented and included in that space was a catalyst for me in eventually realizing that I needed to be open at work. And then I felt able to be so.

All too often queer families would tell me that important information had not been passed on at booking, the right questions were not being asked but the wrong ones were, damaging assumptions were made, and that they felt invisible and, at the same time, exposed.

Since then, and with thanks to them and their voices, I have gone on to work with thousands of families, had the opportunity to facilitate inclusive healthcare training and practice, developed a special interest in supporting LGBTQ and surrogacy grown families and, importantly for me, been happily and proudly visible."

Asking Questions

So, you want to challenge and be aware of your assumptions, but you do also need to occasionally ask personal, potentially sensitive questions. If you were going to ask someone a question, you would first want to be certain that you actually needed the answer in order to best support the individual or family in front of you. Is the question relevant or is it just curiosity on your part? Would you ask a straight/cis person that question (or its equivalent)? Is there a polite (or politer) way to phrase your question?

Remember that you are working with real people, not examples or cases or tokens. We're all individuals, with our own experiences and feelings. It doesn't feel good to get treated like some sort of freaky scientific experiment. Nor is it fair to expect someone to tell you all their personal information just so you can learn about LGBTQ+ parenting. There are other ways of educating yourself.

If you don't need the answer to a particular question, or at least you don't need the answer from this individual you're talking to, perhaps it's better not to ask. Likewise, if you wouldn't dream of asking a heterosexual couple questions such as, "What position were you in when you made your baby?" or "Does the father get jealous because he's not breastfeeding?" then you probably don't want to ask such questions of the LGBTQ+ folks you meet. See Appendix 5 for the kinds of answers you could expect if you're inappropriately nosy with your clients or acquaintances.

How to Ask Questions

As you probably know from your previous experience, asking open questions or gently inviting discussion is generally the best way forward. You can do this without implying you already know the answer or have made assumptions about the person you are dealing with. Try using phrases such as:

Would you like to tell me about…
Could you share…
What do you think about..
It would be helpful for me if you could explain…
To best serve you, I need to understand X. Can you tell me about it?
Apologies if this seems intrusive/personal/sensitive, but I wonder if you can give me some information about…
Could you give me more details about X…

| I feel it would be beneficial if we discussed… |
| I hope it's okay if I ask about X… |

When You Need to Ask Questions

Zoe Faulkner, a heterosexual, cisgender IBCLC, has worked with many LGBTQ+ families. She notes that sometimes you do need to ask questions, which can be quite sensitive or complicated. She advises:

"There are times when the family health history has to be part of the breastfeeding assessment and details are taken into consideration when it comes to identifying possible causes and considering the approach moving forward. When considering allergy, fussy baby, or reflux symptoms, which may be normal baby behavior or may have an allergy component, the genetic history is part of a lactation consultant's assessment.

When taking a history, pay close attention, remember, and document clearly the details shared. An example I have experienced on a number of occasions is when you have a fussy baby, with what are sometimes described as reflux or colicky symptoms. We may be considering the possibility of allergy and, so are looking at the history of allergy in the genetic family.

Whose history are you considering? Which parent/s? What is known, what's unknown? In some families, the birth parent may not be the biological parent. The baby could be conceived using the other mother's egg or via donor egg, as well as donor sperm. When considering genetic factors in baby feeding behaviors and symptoms in a case where the genetics being considered are those of the non-gestational parent, it is important to remember this information, and when relevant to ask the relevant parent about their family history. Then consider this information accordingly and document it accurately."

Questions to Avoid

How did you get/make your child? What clinic did you go to?
So, who's the mother? You know, the *real* mother?
Where's your husband? Where's the father?
What terms do you use? Mommy and Daddy?
Doesn't your child get confused about who you are?
Will the other mother have the next child?
Tell me about the father. How often do you see him? How do you celebrate Father's Day?
What's Dad's medical history? You use the term donor? Well, isn't he still the dad?
Don't your kids want to spend time with their donor? Don't children need a dad?
How did you decide which one of you would get pregnant? Isn't your partner upset that they didn't have the baby?
Can someone who didn't give birth really bond with the baby?
Doesn't your wife get jealous about you breastfeeding? Does your child latch on to your wife's breasts?
What does your family think? Do they approve of your relationship?

I've personally been asked these questions, as have many other LGBTQ+ parents I've spoken to. Let me tell you, it doesn't feel great to be on the receiving end.

A Stor . About Questions and Comments

Jess and Laila, a lesbian couple, conceived using reciprocal IVF.

Jess says that they had to continually come out as gay, to point out that some questions were inappropriate, and to correct professionals about the fact that they were a female-female couple. She explains:

"During the pregnancy, we made it clear to professionals the route we had chosen to conceive and were lucky that we received positive support from practitioners throughout the process.

There were a few occasional comments and remarks such as "Where's the father?" or "Where's your husband from?" or "Please tell the dad to do..." This was corrected and an embarrassed practitioner would quickly apologize.

At times, it did feel we had to continue to state our sexuality to professionals by correcting them or "coming out." Hopefully, in the future, professionals will be more mindful of wording linked to parents and reference to "partners" rather than male labels."

Support for Emotional and Medical Issues

If you are working with LGBTQ+ people as their midwife, doula, doctor, lactation consultant, or other healthcare provider, it is worth being aware of certain medical and emotional issues that may impact on their pregnancy, lactation, or parenting. Some of these have already been discussed in this book, such as induced lactation or using donor milk, so here I just want to briefly mention a few other important topics.

LGBTQ+ people are more likely to have experienced mental health issues, in part because of the homophobia, biphobia, transphobia, and general queerphobia in society, and also potential rejection by their family of origin. This means that some LGBTQ+ people are on antidepressants or other medications. While many, perhaps most, medicines are compatible with pregnancy and breastfeeding/chestfeeding, not all are. Also, someone prone to depression or anxiety may be more likely to suffering with antenatal or postnatal depression. For you, then, listening to how people are feeling and helping them determine and meet their own goals is essential. For example, someone may believe they have to quit breastfeeding before they want to because they need to go on a particular medication, so signposting to information about the safety of medication in breastmilk might be useful.

There are other mental health implications, too. An LGBTQ+ person who has become a parent may become newly aware of how difficult their own childhood was, and so therapy might be beneficial in this case. In addition, a trans man who has become pregnant may be experiencing gender or body dysmorphia again or in a new way, or might have challenging feelings around their decision to get (or not get) surgery, and will require sensitive support.

Whether LGBTQ+ or not, being pregnant, giving birth, and lactating can feel threatening or can bring up difficult feelings. People tend to assume that pregnancy and feeding are something women/females do, and that there is a right way to do these things or to make or have a family. If someone identifies differently or chooses to become pregnant, give birth, or feed in a way that is less common, this may make them question who they are and what their place is in society.

In a family set-up with two or more people, there might be some envy or grief for the one or ones who do not get pregnant or lactate. They might be upset at the way pregnancy or parenthood changes themselves, their partner, or their relationship. They might keep this to themselves or they might talk about it willingly, and they may or may not find that it can cause problems for the relationship, but either way, they may need support with it.

In some LGBTQ+ families, two or more people get pregnant around the same time. While this is the preferred option for some families, it does also mean that the two or more pregnant people cannot necessarily support one another as they could if only one was pregnant, so there may be some stress around this. If one is present for the other's labor and birth, they may feel let down that they will not receive the same level of support in turn from their partner (who will probably be busy with a newborn). If one partner breastfeeds/chestfeeds and the other cannot or does not, this may cause other challenges. On the other hand, they might be able to share the feeding of the babies, which can be a benefit.

Also, in regard to lactation for LGBTQ+ people who are breast-feeding/chestfeeding, they need to consider whether, or when, to start medications for their next round of fertility treatment. They may have to think about what sort of contraception they might want to take, if that is relevant to them, as some types of hormonal birth control can affect lactation.

If you are supporting someone who is trans or non-binary, there are a couple more considerations. In a study of transmasculine individuals' experiences with lactation, it was noted that for those who had chest masculinization surgery or who were considering it:

> Participants did not discuss future infant feeding choices with their surgeons in consultations prior to surgery, and no surgeon brought up the topic. Participants believed that their surgeons subscribed to a binary view of gender, and that pregnancy and chestfeeding would not fit with their surgeons' ideas of what a 'true' transgender man would want to do. To reveal that they were considering future pregnancies or chestfeeding might delay or jeopardize their chance to have chest masculinization surgery (MacDonald et al., 2016).

This is rather shocking and distressing; people are not being given full information about their options before they have surgery, and they are scared to ask for the details themselves. If you are a healthcare provider, you will want to talk through the different types of chest surgery and the impact they can have on feeding with the people you are supporting, just as you would if someone non-LGBTQ+ came in for breast augmentation or reduction.

In general, when it comes to trans or non-binary people:

> Care providers should communicate an understanding of gender dysphoria and transgender identities in order to build patient trust and provide competent care. Further, health care providers need to be knowledge-able about lactation and chest care following chest

masculinization surgery and during binding, regardless of the chosen feeding method and through all stages: before pregnancy, during pregnancy, postpartum, and afterward (MacDonald et al., 2016).

These are just a few of the bigger issues. There are many other challenges, some of which have already been referred to in this book, such as dealing with custody issues for children created in previous relationships or coping with needing to come out frequently in order to explain the family set-up or preferred pronouns.

Some of the Sensitive Issues Pregnancy, Birth, Lactating, and Childrearing Can Raise

Worries about whether these are activities suitable to my gender/sexuality and whether I am doing them "correctly."
Feeling invalidated because I am different than the norm or do things in a way other than the expected.
Body dysmorphia and confusion/pain about the changes my body is experiencing.
Not being recognized as my actual gender/sexuality.
Jealousy or sadness that I could not get pregnant or lactate.
Memories of trauma, such as rejection by family, sexual/ psychological/physical abuse, bullying, and more.
Anger or pain in relation to custody issues.
Stress and lack of support if there are nearly simultaneous pregnancies in a relationship.
Embarrassment or annoyance about having to come out frequently, especially if that information is already listed in the medical notes.
Disappointment or rage in regard to treatment by society, particularly medical professionals.

A Stor, From a Doula About How She Works With LGBTQ+ Clients

Maddie McMahon is a doula, doula course provider, and antenatal educator. She is the author of *Why Doulas Matter* and *Why Mothering Matters,* and she runs https://developingdoulas.co.uk/. She identifies as straight and cisgender. She writes the following:

"I have been a doula for nearly 20 years and in that time have supported a wide variety of families. Living in a city like Cambridge (England) has meant that my client base is incredibly diverse, so I have been lucky enough to work with people from all over the world and from many different backgrounds.

Within this diversity, I have supported rather a lot of families who would describe themselves as part of the LGBTQIA+ community. In particular, I have worked with same-sex parents and trans and non-binary parents.

On a fundamental level, I don't see any reason to change the support I provide just because the parents do not identify as heterosexual or gender normative. All families are unique and will require me to adapt my support to their specific needs. My goal is for all the families I serve to feel seen, heard, and accepted without judgment.

When doulas are supporting families from communities that traditionally have been excluded and discriminated against, we do have to be aware that ignorance and homophobia still exist. These attitudes may impact their maternity care, so I always aim to create an opportunity for conversations about what my clients feel they need from maternity staff and if they feel any disparities in their care. My job is to support them by knowing their rights and helping them navigate the system in a way that will hopefully help them even out those inequities.

However, I have also supported LGBTQIA+ families who have received outstanding care so I am careful not to assume my same-sex and trans clients will have hurtful things said or done to them. Some clients do not wish to discuss this kind of thing with their doula and are just happy they are being treated exactly the same way as a heterosexual couple.

Despite these instances of great care, pregnancy, birth, and new parenthood is an extremely vulnerable time, so even something said in a well-meaning but clumsy way can trigger a lifetime of hurt and feelings of marginalization. So I do offer to work with clients to make plans around how I may be able to protect them or prevent uncomfortable situations. This may involve us talking in great detail about what they may wish me to disclose to staff on their behalf, how they may like to be addressed, or when they would wish me to step in to prevent further upset.

At the end of the day, all anyone wants is to be valued, loved, and celebrated for our unique qualities and talents, and be supported as we work out how best to parent our precious children. Our LGBTQIA+ clients deserve no less."

Meeting Your Clients/Patients Where They Are

When dealing with any patient or client, remember that it's about who they are and what they want and need, rather than about what you think is right. If there are people whose identities, family set-ups, or plans you feel you can't respect or honor, for whatever reason, then it's best to recommend that they work with someone else. Otherwise, it could be an unhappy situation for everyone concerned and that's particularly unfair when someone is vulnerable and emotional, as is often the case when creating a family.

If you do choose to work with someone, ensure that you give them evidence-based information while also respecting their dreams, plans, and decisions. It is your job to meet them where they are, rather than to force them to accept your opinions and preferences. Put simply, it's all about respect and support. Presumably, that's why you chose to become a doctor, midwife, doula, lactation consultant, nurse, etc.; you want to support people and to provide the best quality care you can.

So, ask them who they are and what they want to do and then support them as they work towards it. Recommend appropriate, inclusive books, websites, or baby groups. If you know of anything that's LGBTQ+-specific, pass it on. Show your clients representations of people like them in the media. In short, treat them like the individuals they are and provide tailored help.

Advice on Meeting Your Patients' or Clients' Needs

As mentioned previously in this book, H is a queer/bisexual polyamorous woman who produced and raises her son in a co-parenting relationship. H advises professionals working with LGBTQ+ families as follows:

"I would say that you need to always prioritize and respect what works for your client. Be curious and kind. The sonographers we saw could not believe that we were attending with the father, mother, and the mother's boyfriend. Even the idea of us getting on well enough to do that was wildly out there to them. When we explained that the father and I were just friends (*everyone* assumes we split up while I was pregnant), they were mind-blown. Once we explained, they often thought it was a great set-up.

Keep your mind open and be willing to be flexible about your ways of working. See the positives in alternative arrangements and don't let your preconceived ideas stop you from seeing that a child is in a healthy environment."

Suggestions for Changes We Need to See

> Jess, a lesbian who had her baby via reciprocal IVF with her partner, mentions some of the changes she'd like to see, so professional support could be more beneficial:

> "It would be great to have more representation of gay couples in the media/online or represented in the clinical settings to help professionals understand more about the LGBT community.

> It would also be good to have LGBT Breastfeeding support groups online or in person. Hopefully this could be set up in the future."

Making Mistakes

Hey, guess what? We all make mistakes! We're human and imperfect. It happens.

You might use someone's deadname (the name they were given by their parents but don't use anymore). You might misgender someone. You might get confused about the relationship between the parents and the child. You might tick the wrong box on a form. You might do a whole range of other things. Yes, it can hurt people, but if you didn't do it with malicious intent, then folks usually are pretty understanding. You can make the situation better.

How? It's simple; you apologize. You say you're sorry for making the mistake and you tell them that you'll learn from it and improve. Then you move on.

Easy, right? Let's practice. Say you figure that the two women in your office are sisters, and one of them is just keeping her sister company and helping out with the baby. One of them corrects you and says, "Actually, we're married, and we're the mothers of the child." You don't need to get overly dramatic about it. You can just say, "I'm sorry I made an incorrect assumption. That was a little silly of me. I'll get it right next time." Perhaps you refer to someone who gave birth an hour ago as a "new mother," despite having been told that their preferred pronoun is "he." The man clears his throat, looks up from adoring his new baby, and reminds you of his gender. You can say, "I'm very sorry. I did know that, but I reverted to what I usually say in this situation. I'll do better." In those cases, you've apologized, shown that you understand where you went wrong, and promised to improve.

Few people will hold it against you if you make a mistake. After all, everyone does it. It's the apology and the learning that matter.

Keep Learning

One of the most exciting parts of being alive is continuing to learn and grow. Sometimes this is personal, sometimes it's professional, and sometimes it's both. If you're an ally and/or a professional who works with LGBTQ+ people, I hope you will have learned something from this book. There's still lots more to know. Attending conferences or workshops, reading academic, and popular books and journal articles, learning from activists or advocacy groups, and talking to people are some of the ways you can keep growing. There are times when you can feel yourself expanding with your new knowledge and understanding, and that's absolutely thrilling.

Advice on Continuing to Learn

Zoe Faulkner, a heterosexual, cisgender IBCLC, has worked with many LGBTQ+ families. She explains that professionals should have ongoing professional development and can learn by trying to educate others. Zoe writes:

"Committing to ongoing learning is part of our responsibilities as practitioners. There are many ways to do this, to suit your preferred learning style, including relevant reading, as well as books like this and the related literature, alongside attending conference sessions on the topic.

Lactation consultants and infant feeding roles that involve the education and training of staff or volunteers can support the workforce to be inclusive and facilitate discussion by challenging assumptions and conscious and unconscious bias. The visibility of the diversity of families matters, be it via video clips and choice of images of families, as is using inclusive language, and specific case studies as examples. Seek expert input from others as needed. Ask LGBTQ+ colleagues or families to provide feedback and contribute or share their experiences."

A Few Last Points

Zoe Faulkner, who has been quoted several times in this book, is a cisgender and heterosexual IBCLC, and the chair of Lactation Consultants of Great Britain. She has supported many LGBTQ+ people. Besides what has already been discussed here, she has a few other suggestions, especially regarding how you can make your own practice more inclusive.

Additional Things to Consider from Zoe Faulkner

Create a safe space for the family unit.
Consider the child's right to optimal health when supporting shared feeding or induced lactation.
In record-keeping, describe the family relationships/genetics and roles accurately.
Use inclusive language on your external communication (e.g., website, social media, newsletters).
Consider your responsibilities in light of the UK Equality Act 2010 and Disability Discrimination Act 1995 and the World Health Organization Sustainable Development Goals (or other applicable acts/guidelines).
Consider the potential impact of the intersectionality of additional protected characteristics or support needs.

| Be aware of your own bias, conscious, and unconscious. |
| Ensure that those involved in policy, strategy, and service commissioning and design make it inclusive. |
| Ensure that those involved in teaching, training, and supervision make it inclusive and challenge practice and thinking that is not inclusive. |
| Amplify LGBTQ+ voices in the infant feeding community, including championing representation within feeding support systems. |

Summary

Many LGBTQ+ people find that the treatment they receive in society generally and especially regarding healthcare professionals is less than supportive. That's why I've included this chapter. But really, we could all do more to be better allies to people who are different from us, so it's something everyone is working on in one way or another.

To sum up the suggestions and information here: listen, ask, don't assume, choose your words carefully, don't judge, provide individualized care, say sorry if you get it wrong, and keep developing. This seems obvious and is generally good advice, no matter what the situation.

Something else to remember is that you don't always know from appearances that someone is LGBTQ+ or not, so be sure you are respectful and non-prejudiced in your words and actions with all clients, and indeed with anyone you come across in life. Kindness is something the world needs more of!

Advice in a Nutshell

Listen to what people tell you and repeat their words back to them.
Ask questions politely and respectfully.
Beware of your assumptions.
Treat everyone equally. Don't judge.
Talk to both (or all) parents present. Support both (or all).
Remember that you can't always tell if someone is LGBTQ+.
Provide information and let people make their own decisions.
Be inclusive and welcoming to whatever extent possible.
Apologize if you make a mistake and then learn from it.
Keep learning and growing.
Show people respect and kindness, even if they identify differently than you do or have experiences you don't fully understand.

Conclusion

In this book, we have covered a lot of territory regarding being queer and having a family. We looked at practical information and heard from many people about their own paths and how they feel about them.

We started with queer parenting, considering what's queer about parenting, or how we might parent in our own, queer ways. Isn't it exciting to think that we can parent as we think best? We don't have to do it as our own parents did or as heterosexual or cisgender people do; we're individuals and we can choose our own paths forward.

Then we explored the legal situation in different countries, preparing ourselves for finding out what rights we might, or might not, have, should we decide to make a family. Such rights may have implications for the choices we make.

From there, we talked about all the many, exciting options we LGBTQ+ folks have for family creation, from surrogacy to reciprocal IVF, adoption to co-parenting, and everything in between. I hope you found a method or two that appealed to you and that maybe some of the personal stories inspired you.

We discussed some of the issues around pregnancy and birth, such as antenatal education, baby loss, trauma, and birth preferences, and we considered possibilities for where and how to give birth.

Then we thought about how once you have your baby or child, you may need to plan for recovery, arrange parental leave, ponder what it means to become and be a parent, and prepare for what to say about your lovely queer family. We also looked at all the myriad ways LGBTQ+ people have to choose from when it comes to feeding their babies. Here, too, we heard from a lot of LGBTQ+ people about what they did and how it worked from them.

The last section was aimed specifically at allies and healthcare professionals. Of course, I'm aware that many LGBTQ+ folks themselves are health professionals, just as I am, so I hope you found this chapter useful too. I believe that most people want to do the best they can with their clients, patients, friends, and relatives, but don't always know how, so maybe some tips there will help make our society a little more knowledgeable about LGBTQ+ matters, as well as friendlier to and more supportive of us LGBTQ+ people.

This book mostly covers planning for your family and the early days and years with your new baby or child. I'm aware that there's so much more to think about, such as choosing a school and trying to increase the visibility of LGBTQ+ families and topics in your child's education, deciding whether to have another child, navigating friendships with other parents, finding your religious/spiritual home as an LGBTQ+ family, parenting through tantrums and rebellion, LGBTQ+ communities, teaching your child about sexuality and gender, and much more. That may have to wait for a follow-up book! For now, I hope you found the information and personal experiences shared here beneficial as you take steps towards forming your family.

Let's remember that many of us LGBTQ+ people didn't believe we would be able to have children. Maybe we were even told when we came out that we shouldn't; a relative said to me in some disgust, "People like you don't have kids!" Maybe we live in places where it is hard to create families as LGBTQ+ folks. So, however you make your unique rainbow family, maybe we can take a moment to be grateful. LGBTQ+ parenting looks different for each queer person and family, but for most of us, having kids is an intentional, conscious, challenging choice, one that takes quite a lot of work, and may involve dealing with stereotypes, prejudice, and many hindrances. But we're here, we're queer, and we're parents! How amazing is that?

A Stor, of Gratitude

Lesbian couple Deb and Perse created a blended and extended family, moving from the UK, where they didn't have great experiences, to New Zealand, where they did. Deb sums it all up when she writes:

"We are incredibly lucky and grateful to have been able to welcome our two new additions to our blended rainbow whānau (family) and to have experienced such loving and compassionate care during my two birth-givings. We still get the occasional astonished look from passers-by in the street as we walk together, hand-in-hand with our babies in tow, and we are often told how "similar" we look (we don't!) by people too used to differentiating parents by gender presentation. That said, we have never encountered any animosity, and are now fairly well-known locally as "the lesbian couple with the babies."

We definitely feel that we are contributing to the normalization of and raising the visibility of the existence of same-sex families in our conservative, rural hometown, particularly within the religious communities who run most of the play groups here. In fact, the most frequent expression of confusion regarding us and our babies happens when we are out with our older daughter (18 years old), who is invariably assumed to be their mom, and us their grannies (for the record, we are 38 and 45 years old)."

Another Stor, of Gratitude

B.J. and Hi are a queer couple with two young children (yes, this is the same B.J. who has written this book). B.J. writes:

"If we had lived in a different time or different place, we wouldn't have been able to build our amazing family. I feel so lucky to have had the privilege to have access to legal rights and to fertility treatment, and to have had the money to pay for this treatment. I feel so lucky to have gone on this journey with my wonderful wife.

We LGBTQ+ people aren't free to be ourselves everywhere in the world yet. So, though I'm happy to be me and to have the life I do, the fight isn't over. Let's make parenthood a possibility for all queers, all over the world."

In closing, I want to say good luck to you as you plan your family and as you parent. Enjoy your beautiful LGBTQ+ family!

References

Huge thanks to all the people who shared their personal and/or professional stories. I can't cite them in the traditional way, but please recognize that they provided important information for this book and deserve to be considered references and resources.

American Experience. (n.d.). *Milestones in the American gay rights movement.* PBS. https://www.pbs.org/wgbh/americanexperience/features/stonewall-milestones-american-gay-rights-movement/

Arneson, K. (2021, June 29). *The U.S. is the only rich nation offering no national paid parental-leave programme. Why is that – and could it change?* BBC. https://www.bbc.com/worklife/article/20210624-why-doesnt-the-us-have-mandated-paid-maternity-leave

Ask Lenore (n.d.). *Induced lactation.*https://www.asklenore.info/breastfeeding/induced_lactation/gn_protocols.shtml

Australian Breastfeeding Association and Rainbow Families New South Wales. (2021). *Breastfeeding, chest feeding and human milk feeding: Supporting LGBTQIA+ Families.* https://d3n8a8pro7vhmx.cloudfront.net/rainbowfamilies/pages/958/attachments/original/1626606574/ABA_RF_Booklet_Web.pdf?1626606574

British Broadcasting Corporation. (2021, February 10). *Brighton NHS Trust introduces new trans-friendly terms.* https://www.bbc.co.uk/news/uk-england-sussex-56007728

Brown, A. (2019). *Why breastfeeding grief and trauma matter.* Pinter & Martin.

Brown, A. (2021). *Let's talk about feeding your baby.* Pinter & Martin.

Caron, C. (2020, June 1). Gay couples can teach straight people a thing or two about arguing. *New York Times.* https://www.nytimes.com/2020/06/01/parenting/relationship-advice-gay-straight.html

Carr, J. (2021, August 9). *Same-sex parents battle for inclusive paperwork for baby.* BBC. https://www.bbc.co.uk/news/uk-england-devon-58071558

Compton, J. (2019, February 7). *LGBTQ families poised for 'dramatic growth,' national survey finds.* NBC News. https://www.nbcnews.com/feature/nbc-out/lgbtq-families-poised-dramatic-growth-national-survey-finds-n968776

Cornell University Public Policy Research Portal. (n.d.). *What does the scholarly research say about the well-being of children with gay or lesbian parents?*

https://whatweknow.inequality.cornell.edu/topics/lgbt-equality/
what-does-the-scholarly-research-say-about-the-wellbeing-of-children-
with-gay-or-lesbian-parents/

de la Cretaz, B. (2016, August 23). What it's like to chestfeed. *The Atlantic*.
https://www.theatlantic.com/health/archive/2016/08/chestfeeding/497015/

Deahl, J. (2021, September 22). *Surrogacy is absolutely what I want to do*. BBC.
https://www.bbc.co.uk/news/uk-58639955

Dettwyler, K. (1997). *A natural age of weaning*. Health e-Learning. https://www.
health-e-learning.com/articles/A_Natural_Age_of_Weaning.pdf

Droplet. (2021). Downloads. https://firstdroplets.com/downloads/

Epstein, B. J. (2013). *Are the kids all right? Representations of LGBTQ characters in
children's and young adult literature*. Hammer On Press.

Epstein, B. J., & Chapman, E. L. (2021). *International LGBTQ+ literature for children
and young adults*. Anthem Press.

Fairtlough, A. (2008). Growing up with a lesbian or gay parent: Young people's
perspectives. *Health and Social Care in the Community, 16*(5), 521–528.

Family Equality. (2020). *Facts about LGBTQ+ Families*. https://www.familyequality.
org/resources/facts-about-lgbtq-families/

FFLAG. (n.d.) *LGBT+ parenting*. https://www.fflag.org.uk/portfolio-item/lgbtplus-
parenting/

First Steps Nutrition. (2021). *Infant milks: Information for parents & carers*. https://
www.firststepsnutrition.org/parents-carers

Freeman, T., Zadeh, S., Smith, V., & Golombok, S. (2016). Disclosure of sperm
donation: A comparison between solo mother and two-parent families with
identifiable donors. *Reproductive BioMedicine Online, 33*, 592–600.

Fried, D. (2017). My first time breastfeeding my daughter. *The Stranger*. https://
www.thestranger.com/queer-issue-2017/2017/06/21/25225867/my-
first-time-breastfeeding-my-daughter

Gates, G. J. (2011). *How many people are lesbian, gay, bisexual, and transgender?*
UCLA Williams Institute. https://williamsinstitute.law.ucla.edu/publications/
how-many-people-lgbt/

Gates, G. J. (2013). *LGBT parenting in the United States*. UCLA Williams Institute.
https://williamsinstitute.law.ucla.edu/publications/lgbt-parenting-us/

Goldberg, A. E., Kashy, D. A., & Smith, J. Z. (2012). Gender-typed play behavior in early
childhood: Adopted children with lesbian, gay, and heterosexual parents.
Sex Roles, 67(9-10), 503–515. https://doi.org/10.1007/s11199-012-0198-3

Goldberg, S. K., & Conron, K. J. (2018). How many same-sex couples in the U.S. are
raising children? *UCLA Williams Institute*. https://williamsinstitute.law.ucla.
edu/publications/same-sex-parents-us/

Gottman, J. M., Levenson, R. W., Swanson, C., Swanson, K., Tyson, R., & Yoshimoto, D. (2003). Observing gay, lesbian and heterosexual couples' relationships: Mathematical modeling of conflict interaction. *Journal of Homosexuality, 45*(1). https://www.johngottman.net/wp-content/uploads/2011/05/Observing-Gay-Lesbian-and-heterosexual-Couples-Relationships-Mathematical-modeling-of-conflict-interactions.pdf

Gov.uk. (n.d.). *Apply for a gender recognition certificate.* https://www.gov.uk/apply-gender-recognition-certificate

Green, H., & Riddington, A. (2020). *Perinatal care for trans and non-binary people.* https://www.bsuh.nhs.uk/maternity/wp-content/uploads/sites/7/2021/01/MP005-Perinatal-Care-for-Trans-and-Non-Binary-People.pdf

Harman, T., & Wakeford, A. (2016). *The microbiome effect.* Pinter & Martin.

Hearts Milk Bank (2012). *FAQ.* https://heartsmilkbank.org/faqs/

Hicks, S. (2005). Is gay parenting bad for kids? Responding to the 'very idea of difference' in research on lesbian and gay parents. *Sexualities, 8*(2), 153–168.

Hinde, K. (2016). Evolving motherhood: When to wean, part I. *International Milk Genomics. https://milkgenomics.org/article/evolving-motherhood-when-to-wean-part-i/*

Jenkins, I. (2021). *Three dads and a baby.* Cleis Press.

Johnson, S. M., & O'Connor, E. (2002). *The gay baby boom.* New York University Press.

King, K. (2020). *Why baby loss matters.* Pinter & Martin.

Kleeman, J. (2021, September 25). The great sperm heist: 'They were playing with people's lives'. *The Guardian.* https://www.theguardian.com/lifeandstyle/2021/sep/25/the-great-sperm-heist-they-were-playing-with-peoples-lives

Kuvalanka, K. A., Leslie, L. A., & Radina, R. (2013). Coping with sexual stigma: Emerging adults with lesbian parents reflect on the impact of heterosexism and homophobia during their adolescence. *Journal of Adolescent Research.* http://miamioh.edu/chs/_files/documents/fsw/research/kuvalanka-leslie-radina-2013.pdf

Lawrie, E. (2021). *Lesbian couple challenge NHS over 'discriminatory' fertility policy.* BBC. https://www.bbc.co.uk/news/health-59206378

MacDonald, T., Noel-Weiss, J., West, D., Walks, M., Biener, M., Kibbe, A., & Myler, E. (2016). Transmasculine individuals' experiences with lactation, chestfeeding, and gender identity: A qualitative study. *BMC Pregnancy and Childbirth, 16.* https://bmcpregnancychildbirth.biomedcentral.com/articles/10.1186/s12884-016-0907-y

Milner, J., & Arezina, J. (2018). The accuracy of ultrasound estimation of fetal weight in comparison to birth weight: A systematic review. *Ultrasound, 26*(1), 32–41.

Oakley, S. (2021). *Why tongue-tie matters.* Pinter & Martin.

Office of National Statistics. (2020). *Sexual orientation, UK: 2019.* https://www.ons.gov.uk/peoplepopulationandcommunity/culturalidentity/sexuality/bulletins/sexualidentityuk/2019

Oxford Population Health. (2021). *The birthplace cohort study: Key findings.* University of Oxford NPEU. https://www.npeu.ox.ac.uk/birthplace/results#main

Reardon, S. (2019). Do C-section babies need mum's microbes? Trials tackle controversial idea. *Nature.* https://www.nature.com/articles/d41586-019-02348-3

Ruhe, N. (2015, July 8). *The battle over breast milk: For-profit milk banks versus non-profit milk banks.* MedCity News. https://medcitynews.com/2015/07/breast-milk-milk-banks/

Sale, A. (2021). *Let's talk about hard things.* Scribe.

Silsby, G. (2001, May 30). *Sociology: Study examines gender roles of children with gay parents.* USCNews. https://news.usc.edu/5011/Sociology-Study-examines-gender-roles-of-children-with-gay-parents/

Solomon, A. (2012). *Far from the tree.* Chatto and Windus.

Spiegelhalter, D. (2015, April 5). Is 10% of the population really gay? *The Observer.* https://www.theguardian.com/society/2015/apr/05/10-per-cent-population-gay-alfred-kinsey-statistics

Stacey, J., & Biblarz, T. J. (2001). (How) does the sexual orientation of parents matter? *American Sociological Review, 66*(2), 159–183. https://doi.org/10.2307/2657413

Stanford University. (n.d). *Hand expression of breastmilk.* https://med.stanford.edu/newborns/professional-education/breastfeeding/hand-expressing-milk.html

Stonewall. (n.d.). *Key dates for lesbian, gay, bi and trans equality.* https://www.stonewall.org.uk/key-dates-lesbian-gay-bi-and-trans-equality

Subudhi, S., & Sriraman, N. (2021). Islamic beliefs about milk kinship and donor human milk in the United States. *Pediatrics, 47*(2), doi: 10.1542/peds.2020-0441. https://pubmed.ncbi.nlm.nih.gov/33483451/

Woodstein, B.J. (2022). *The portrayals of breastfeeding in literature.* Anthem Press.

Silverberg, C., & Smyth, F. (2013). *What makes a baby.* Seven Stories.

Wiessinger, D., West, D., & Pitman, T. (2013). *The womanly art of breastfeeding.* Pinter & Martin.

World Health Organization. (2020). *Children: improving survival and well-being.* https://www.who.int/news-room/fact-sheets/detail/children-reducing-mortality

Yate, Z. (2020). *When breastfeeding sucks.* Pinter & Martin.

Young, C. (2016). *Why breastfeeding matters.* Pinter & Martin.

Appendices

In the main part of this book, I referred to some extra information, such as how to work with a known donor or how to reply to personal questions. You'll find all that info here!

Appendix 1: Ovulation Chart

When tracking ovulation, it is certainly possible to simply use an app on your phone, where you enter data about your periods, or to buy commercial ovulation strips. The strips are like pregnancy tests in that you pee on them and they give you information: in this case, whether you're ovulating. However, they only tell you when you are ovulating, rather than also helping you see that you're in the run-up to ovulation. Knowing you're ovulating is useful, especially if you happen to have sperm on-tap (i.e., if you have a male partner or if your sperm donor lives nearby), ready to drop everything to inseminate you.

But that may not be your situation, or you may be someone who prefers to have more knowledge about your body or control over what's happening. So that's why charting your cycle may make more sense for you. You'll be paying close attention to certain key features of your body—your cycle generally, when you are menstruating, your temperature, your cervical mucus—so that you can predict when you will ovulate. This is helpful so you can make travel arrangements for yourself or your sperm donor or so you can order sperm to be shipped to you. It's deflating to pay for sperm or to travel to see your donor only to realize that you aren't ovulating and your likelihood of getting pregnant is low.

Ovulation takes place around two weeks before menstruation, but this does vary depending on how long someone's cycle is.

Generally, people are most fertile in the couple of days before ovulation and the day of ovulation, but again, this can differ between people. You will typically notice increased amounts of slippery cervical mucus (sometimes called discharge) and usually your temperature will rise slightly. You might wish to track your mucus and temperature throughout the month, so you can tell when there have been changes. When you take your temperature, you should do it right when you wake up in the morning, before you get out of bed or move around. Consider keeping the thermometer and your chart next to the bed.

Some people also notice breast tenderness, increased sexual desire, changes to the feel of their cervix, or abdominal tenderness when they are ovulating. These are also bits of data that you can use when tracking your fertility.

When you have sex or inseminate, you can tick the appropriate box in the chart. Many people like to try several times during their window of fertility.

As the months pass, you will figure out the cycle and patterns that are specific to you. It isn't always as easy as just inseminating exactly 2 weeks before your period is due. On the other hand, who knows? You might be one of the lucky ones who gets pregnant on your first attempt.

If you are using a fertility clinic, they will track and possibly control your cycles carefully, generally using a combination of medications and ultrasounds. They'll also be likely to tell you when to use a so-called trigger shot, which contains hormones, to release your eggs. You may still want to track your cycle for your own knowledge, however.

CHART

MONTH

Temperature scale (left and right margins):
99.1, 99, 98.9, 98.8, 98.7, 98.6, 98.5, 98.4, 98.3, 98.2, 98.1, 98, 97.9, 97.8, 97.7, 97.6, 97.5, 97.4, 97.3, 97.2, 97.1, 97, 96.9, 96.8, 96.7, 96.6, 96.5, 96.4, 96.3

Day columns: 1–38

DAY
DATE
PERIOD
MUCUS
INSEM
OTHER
COMMENTS

Appendix 2: Discussions with a Known Donor or Surrogate

If your situation involves someone donating their sperm informally or someone loaning their uterus to you it makes sense for those involved to sit down and discuss how they want and expect their relationship to be. It's important to recognize that feelings and wishes can change over the course of a child's life and that obviously the child will have their own feelings about the situation as they get older. Nonetheless, it helps if the donor/surrogate and the intended parents know what their expectations are from the beginning.

It can even be helpful to formalize the discussions into a contract. Although the contract wouldn't be legally binding, it can still be beneficial to have the plans written down. In case there is a conflict, you can take the contract with you to a counsellor, lawyer, or ombudsman, and use it as a starting-point for conversation and negotiation.

Note that egg donation has to happen through a clinic and while the donor might be a friend or relative—which would mean discussing these things—it is often more likely to be an unknown donor (at least until the conceived child turns eighteen). Still, this list can easily be adapted for an egg donor or a surrogate.

So, what kind of things might you want to include in your discussions and contract?

An Initial List of Possible Topics

How will the child be made? Will it be through intercourse, or will the donor provide sperm at home or at a clinic?
How many times will you try at home before considering a swap to a fertility clinic?
How many attempts do you want to have, regardless of where they take place?
How many children is the donor willing to help you make? What happens if they change their mind?
Will the donor give up any legal rights they are entitled to?
Will the donor contribute any money to the child's upbringing?
Will the child/children know who the donor/surrogate is?
Will there be continued contact through the child's childhood?
What name will the donor/surrogate be known by?
If this is about a surrogate, will they be paid? Which costs will be covered?
Will the surrogate provide human milk? For how long?
Approximately how often can the donor/surrogate expect to receive pictures and email updates, if at all?
Approximately how often will the donor/surrogate have visits with the child, if any? Will they be supervised by the parents? Who will pay for any visits that require travel?
Will the donor/surrogate have any overnight stays with the child/children or be able to take them on trips?
Will the donor/surrogate be involved in the child or children's upbringing at all?
Who will make decisions about issues such as names, schooling, religion, parenting standards, and so on?
Who would become the guardian if something happened to the legal parent/s? Would the donor/surrogate be involved as a guardian in that situation?

Would the donor's or surrogate's family be involved at all?
Would they be known to the child as grandparents, aunts,
uncles, etc.?"

What else matters to you as individuals and collectively that
would be important to discuss?

Appendix 3: Birth Preferences

If you or your partner have gotten pregnant, you will want to start thinking about where and how to give birth. Sometimes this is referred to as a birth plan but given that it's hard to carry out a birth exactly as you wish, I like to use the term birth preferences. In other words, you can prefer, but it's difficult to plan for birth.

Think through what you would prefer to happen and why. Take your time and don't worry if you change your mind.

You might wish to write two or more birth preferences lists, such as one for a home birth and one for the hospital. Even if you are planning on a home birth, for example, you might find that you wish to transfer to the hospital in the end. Conversely, you might plan on going to the hospital and then find you want to stay home. As an example of birth preferences changing, I was the doula at a birth that started at home. The pregnant person had been unsure about whether they wanted their mother there. The mother did come to the house during early labor and continually made unhelpful and sometimes downright annoying comments. This stressful atmosphere stalled labor. My client didn't want to offend their mother by asking her to leave—but please note that if ever there's a time when you can offend people and not care, it's while you're giving birth—so actually chose to swap to the hospital, where only one birth partner was allowed. The mother stayed home, and my client went off to the hospital to give birth in peace.

So, having clear preferences can help your partner, the midwives, doctors, doula, and anyone else there during labor.

Some Things to Include in Your
Birth Preferences Document

Your name.
Your partner's name/partners' names, if applicable.
Address.
Phone numbers.
Names of people who will be at the birth (including a doula, any partners, any relatives or friends, any older children, etc.) and their phone numbers.
Names of people you do not want at the birth (i.e., if you don't want students present, or if there is a relative who you antici-pate might try to join in but whose presence is not desired).
Where the birth will take place.
Your preferred language (i.e., if you want people to say "surges" and not "contractions," or "chestfeeding" instead of "breastfeeding").
The sort of atmosphere you want to have (consider candles, lighting, aromatherapy, music, images, and so forth).
If there is anything important for the people present to know about you medically (such as allergies, epilepsy, diabetes, etc., even if this is already listed in your notes).
If something happened during a previous experience giving birth that is relevant (such as a tear that means you need extra perineal support or a trauma that you wish to avoid repeating).
Any techniques or approaches you would like to use during the birth (such as hypnobirthing, a TENS machine, or back massage).
Whether you want internal examinations and/or fetal monitor-ing, and whether you want to be told what the findings are.
What positions you might like to use.
Whether you want to use a birth pool, a birthing stool, a shower, a birth support rope, and so on.

What sort of pain relief you want, if any, and whether you want to be offered it or if you prefer to ask for it yourself.
If you are open to the use of forceps or vacuum/ventouse.
Who can speak for you if you feel unable to speak.
Who you would like to receive the baby (in the absence of a medical emergency).
Whether you want someone to announce the baby's sex and, if so, who.
When you would like the umbilical cord to be cut and by whom.
How you want to birth the placenta (if you want the injection, for example) and if you want to keep the placenta for encapsulation or burying.
What you would like to happen immediately post-birth (for instance, a "golden hour" where you are skin-to-skin with the baby, or support with latching).
Whether you want the baby to be given vitamin K and, if so, whether orally or by injection.
How you plan to feed your baby.
Anything else that you want people to know about your ideal birth.

Appendix 4: Hospital Bag

If you are planning on a hospital birth or if there is a chance you might end up in the hospital, you will want to be organized in terms of getting everything ready in advance that you might need while in the hospital.

However, if you do forget something, it's not the end of the world. The hospital might have it, or there might be a shop in the hospital or nearby that has it, or your birth partner can go get it from home or elsewhere. It may not be that essential anyway.

You'll want to get your bags ready in plenty of time, so you aren't in early labor, rushing around your home, trying to remember what you needed to gather. Don't forget that babies don't usually come on their due date; they can come early, so be ready.

By the way, if you're traveling somewhere to adopt a child, this list might be useful to you as well. Some adoptive parents do breast-feed/chestfeed their babies, so nursing tops or breast pads could be needed, but even if that's not your situation, you will need changes of clothing, money, phones and chargers, toiletries, and so forth.

Suggested Items for the Pregnant Person's Hospital Bag

ID.
Your hospital notes.
Your birth plans.
Multiple changes of clothing (for labor, for recovery, for going home).
Multiple changes of large, comfortable underpants.
Bikini top for the birthing pool, if desired.
Hair bands or clips, as needed.
Maternity pads (not the same as sanitary pads).
Dressing gown and slippers.
Shampoo, conditioner, soap, lotion, deodorant, lip balm, toothbrush, toothpaste, and other toiletries.
Towels.
Books, magazines, music.
Phone and charger.
Portable battery.
Camera.
TENS machine, if using.
Food and drink.
Silicone or bamboo straws and sports-type bottle.
Nursing tops and bras.
Breast pads.
Fan.
Pillows.
Candles, photos, aromatherapy oils, or any other items to relax you or remind you of home.

Suggested Items for the Birth Partner's Hospital Bag

Remember: You might be at the hospital for a while, so bring plenty of things to nourish and entertain yourself and to keep yourself feeling fresh, so you can focus on supporting the birthing person.

ID.
A copy of the birth plans.
Phone and charger.
Portable battery.
Camera.
Multiple changes of clothing.
Swimsuit (if you plan to get into the shower or birthing pool, too).
Toiletries.
Food and drink.
Money.
Books, magazines, music.
Phone numbers of people you might need to call to share news with.

Suggested Items for the Baby's Hospital Bag

Nappies/diapers (cloth or disposable).
Cloths or wipes or cotton wool.
Muslins/burp cloths.
Multiple changes of clothing (including vests/onesies, bodysuits, sleepsuits, etc.).
Warm cardigan or coat for going home in.
A hat (though you might be given one at the hospital).
Blanket.
A car seat.

Appendix 5: Handling Nosy Questions and Personal Comments

You'd hope all people would treat one another with respect and kindness. Alas, that's not the world we live in. Not yet anyway.

Unfortunately, it's inevitable that LGBTQ+ families will arouse interest. Sometimes people are genuinely curious and have never considered how LGBTQ+ folks produce children. Some are just chatty and talk without thinking too much about how what they are saying might be received. Other times, there are people who don't understand or accept your family. So you may get some odd, offensive, or inappropriate remarks or queries. This can be startling at times, and you might not always think of a good reply immediately (it's the so-called *l'esprit d'escalier* problem, where you come up with a snappy remark later).

While there are occasions when you feel like giving people information—whether you want to educate them, or because they are people you trust, or because you're the type who loves to share, or for other reasons—there will also be times when you don't want to tell the whole world your personal story. You might give people a surprised look and that could be enough to stop them from digging into your business, or you might choose to change the subject, but there are times when some sort of rejoinder is called for.

So, here are a few suggestions that you can keep in mind to use when you are faced with a prying or rude interlocutor. I've used many of them myself at different times! Beware that some of them seem quite obnoxious, but then again, sometimes a situation requires that. Actually, I've found that a sharp reply can make people stop and consider what exactly they're saying. If someone asks, "What does your family think?" and you respond, "What does **your** family think?" then they might recognize that it could, in fact, be a sensitive topic that isn't something you want to talk about right now, if ever.

Suggested Responses to Nosy or
Inappropriate Comments and Questions

Why do you ask?
Why are you interested in this topic?
What makes you say that?
What do you think about it?
What do you mean by that question/comment?
Sorry, I don't understand why you're getting at.
That's my children's story/business to tell, if they choose to do so when they're older.
Ah, I could tell you, but then I'd have to kill you!
If I only knew!
How did I get pregnant? Oh, I slipped and fell on a penis!
I didn't realize I was pregnant! How shocking!
Do we need to have a biology lesson?
Have you told your parents that you're straight/cisgender?
What does your family think?
What position were you in when you made your babies?
Actually, we're both the mothers/fathers.
I try not to talk about my personal life at work [or wherever you currently are].
My personal life is none of your concern.
I'm sorry, but this isn't really the time for this conversation.
It's a long story, and this isn't the right time/place.
I'd rather not discuss that.
This isn't a conversation I feel comfortable having.
Thanks for your interest, but I prefer not to talk about that right now.
This isn't really appropriate to discuss.
Oh, that's pretty personal.
You may not have realized that that's a very intimate/sensitive topic.
Your question/comment has upset me. Could we change the subject?

I'd prefer to talk about something else.
Well, I can talk to you about this in general, without giving specifics about my family.
Here are some possible ways for LGBTQ+ people to have produced children…
What do you know about this topic already?
I'd love to hear about your experiences. What's your story?
Can I recommend a book/website for you, if you'd like to learn about that?
Dr. Google might be able to answer that for you.

Appendix 6: Resources

There is a lot more to be said about all of the subjects discussed in this book, as well as adjacent ones. For example, you can find memoirs about people's parenting journeys, there are books about being LGBTQ+ and religious, or about being LGBTQ+ in particular countries, or you can get encyclopedic tomes (or articles, for that matter) about any aspect of pregnancy, birth, and parenting. You'll also be able to find websites and social media groups devoted to just about any approach you can imagine. Do be careful about what you read and determine whether it's trustworthy. Be sure to go with a combination of science, common sense, and your instincts when it comes to deciding what you want to do.

I generally recommend evidence-based books by reputable authors and publishers, so you know research supports what you are being told. Many books published by Praeclarus (in the US) and Pinter and Martin (in the UK) are well worth a read. As ever, though, be aware that not all authors or texts are fully committed to diversity and inclusivity.

The references list for this book might be a good place to start and also here are a few texts on some of the topics I have discussed. Of course, there are many more you could find, so go to the bookstore or the library and see what appeals to you.

A Few Reading Suggestions

Please note that most are not LGBTQ+- specific.

Pregnancy

Polyamory and Pregnancy by Jessica Burde

Pregnancy and Birth by Kaz Cooke

Miscarriage and Other Baby Loss

Why Baby Loss Matters by Kay King

Birth

Dynamic Positions in Birth by Margaret Jowitt

Let's Talk About Preparing for Your Baby's Birth by Jackie Kietz

Doulas

Why Doulas Matter by Maddie McMahon

Breastfeeding/Chestfeeding

The Positive Breastfeeding Book by Amy Brown

Breastfeeding Doesn't Need to Suck by Kathleen Kendall-Tackett

Where's the Mother? Stories from a Transgender Dad by Trevor MacDonald

Combination-Feeding

Mixed Up by Lucy Ruddle

Recovery from Birth

Why Postnatal Recovery Matters by Sophie Messager

Sleep

Safe Infant Sleep by James McKenna

Being an LGBTQ+ Ally

The Savvy Ally by Jeannie Gainsburg

Other

The Microbiome Effect by Toni Harman and Alex Wakeford

Let's Talk About the First Year of Parenting by Amy Brown

When Breastfeeding Sucks by Zainab Yate

Websites

https://breastfeeding.support/ (on infant feeding)

https://www.breastfeedingnetwork.org.uk/drugs-factsheets/ (on drugs in breastmilk)

https://www.breastfeedingaversion.com/ (on aversion, including a free support course)

https://www.basisonline.org.uk/ (UK-based website on infant sleep)

https://cosleeping.nd.edu/ (U.S.-based website on infant sleep)

https://www.youtube.com/channel/UCNTbZy88kyTvZkIS diCi00w (Savvy Ally Action, for information on being a better LGBTQ+ ally)

Printed in Great Britain
by Amazon